THE IMPORTANCE OF BEING ETHICAL

Essays on Ethics: A Solicitor's Perspective

John Spencer

Foreword

By Andrew Hopper QC

In this admirable series of essays John Spencer explores the extent to which this nation has – in moral and ethical terms – lost its way; in business, but also in sport, in media and entertainment, in the behaviour of public authorities such as the police, and in politics.

At a time in which there is something of a mania for regulation, and extended debates about the extent and detail of regulation, one is inclined to overlook the difference between "the rules" and ethics. They are very different concepts.

I have been fortunate to know John for many years. One statement can be made with absolute certainty:

John Spencer is an honourable man.

In this book we see through the eyes of an honest and honourable man, with a sense of bewilderment – but by no means a naïve bewilderment – how we have come to tolerate, if not to applaud unethical behaviour, when we would normally conclude that right-thinking people would view that same behaviour with abhorrence. That tolerance of cheating, lying or other immoral behaviour leads to a general lowering of standards to the prejudice of society as a whole.

Whether it is the cheating sportsman, who can be praised for "getting away with it" – and seemingly the more skilful and charismatic the player, the more his (invariably his, rather than her) cheating is tolerated – or in the cut-throat approach to competition in such television programmes as *The Apprentice*, where invented CVs are seemingly rewarded with success, rather than having the expected consequence of complete loss of trust, or in the exposure of lies and 'covering up' by police, or through the appalling behaviour of our politicians as exemplified by the Parliamentary expenses scandal, we see the malaise caused by a loss of ethical standards.

Perhaps the expenses scandal gives the most insight: whether Members of Parliament were ultimately prosecuted and convicted of outright fraud, or 'only' embarrassed into repaying large sums of money they should never have claimed in the first place, they all spoke with one voice: they had "done nothing wrong" – that is, they had, with varying degrees of success, sought to apply the letter of the then Green Book, the generously worded guide to expenses claims, while wholly losing sight of the overriding principle that the behaviour of MPs should be above reproach; that they should behave honourably.

After all, every statement in the House of Commons by a member to another is addressed through the Speaker to "my Honourable friend" (or Right Honourable if the addressee is a Privy Councillor), yet in the scramble for money that oft-repeated phrase had been forgotten. If, instead of being allowed to claim that they had done nothing wrong according to "the rules", MPs had been challenged as to whether what they had done was consistent with their honour and integrity; whether what they had done could possibly be justified by any ethical or moral code, there might have been more embarrassing silences or even less persuasive answers.

In the final essay we see John's decades of personal experience, in relation to claims for damages for personal injuries by injured members of the public, brought to bear on the wider debate. We see that the insurance lobby's misleading mantra about the existence of a "compensation culture", and its claims that whiplash injuries are a British invention, are fallacies, and simply a public relations exercise for the increase in profits, though apparently swallowed whole by our current politicians.

It is a sobering read, but hopefully our society is not altogether beyond hope, and this book will help to stimulate debate and encourage more ethical behaviours. I commend it.

Andrew Hopper QC
August 2014

Introduction

It is curious – that physical courage should be so common in the world, and moral courage so rare – Mark Twain.

This book's title is a play on Oscar Wilde's well-known play, *The Importance of Being Earnest.* I will explain why in this brief introduction.

In Wilde's play, Victorian notions of respectability and duty are satirized. Gwendolen Fairfax is in love with a man she knows as Ernest. In fact, Ernest is the alter ego of Jack Worthing, who was found in a handbag in the cloakroom of a London railway station by a Mr Thomas Cardew. Despite Jack's inauspicious start in life, he grows up among the landed gentry and is known as a pillar of the community in Hertfordshire, where he has a country estate. He finds his everyday life stultifying, and to escape it engineers a remarkable ruse: a disreputable brother called Ernest, whom he is always having to save from some calamity or other. Ernest, of course, does not exist.

Jack is a hypocrite, a man at ease with his deception. He wants to be perceived as upright and respectable, and has no qualms about his double identity. Gwendolen is no less preoccupied by the veneer of appearances. Obsessed with finding a husband whose name is Ernest – the name "inspires absolute confidence", says Gwendolen – she is unable to see through the deceit of Jack/Ernest.

The quality of being 'earnest' is uppermost in Wilde's mind. For him, being earnest meant inhabiting a world of false truths, smugness and complacency, a world in which so long as things appear to be alright, then they must be alright. Hence the play's most famous quote, uttered by the snobbish Lady Bracknell to Jack/Ernest: "To lose one parent, Mr Worthing, may be regarded as misfortune; to lose both looks like carelessness."

The play's denouement reveals that appearances are not to be relied upon; that to probe beneath the surface is to find a different story and, in fact, the truth.

The play is 'classic Oscar Wilde', in that his works are as paradoxical as they are amusing. As well as this, it is as relevant today as it was when it was first performed over 100 years ago, on 14 February 1895 at St James's Theatre in London. Wilde still manages to shine a light on the hypocrisy which has come to permeate so many sectors of society.

In law and in other arenas, from politics and journalism to sport and popular entertainment, appearances often disguise a worrying, not to say downright unpleasant reality. So long as everything seems to be OK, we ignore standards of professionalism and ethical rigour. But if we strip away the veneer, we find Jack Worthing, and Gwendolen Fairfax, to be alive and well.

This book is a call to arms for those who believe in sound ethical principles and professionalism, in the concept of putting duty before profit, and for those who, like Jack Worthing, may prove to be Ernest after all. I have selected five areas which I do not so much analyse as reflect on: sport, popular entertainment, public life (in particular, the police and politics), big business and the personal injury (PI) claims sector. In each, I take what is consciously a broad brush view, though readers will find that the book grows more focused and specific by its close. At the end, I bring the seemingly diverse threads together, in the hope that this book will have resonance for anyone who cares about the British public – especially those who believe that it is, after all, important to be ethical.

Essay 1: Ethics in Sport

In the end, it's the extra effort that separates a winner from second place. But winning takes a lot more than that, too. It starts with complete command of the fundamentals. Then it takes desire, determination, discipline, and self-sacrifice. And finally, it takes a great deal of love, fairness and respect for your fellow man. Put all these together, and even if you don't win, how can you lose? – Jesse Owens

Getting away with it

"Good luck to him. He got away with one."

That was the verdict of Ian Botham, one of England's best ever cricketers, on Stuart Broad electing to stand his ground during the first test of The Ashes series in 2013. Broad was caught at first slip by Michael Clarke, following a delivery by the young Australian hotshot, Ashton Agar. The batsman clearly nicked the ball and Clarke was alert to its flight, despite a deflection off Brad Haddin, the Australian wicket-keeper. Under the laws of the game, Broad was out.

Except that the rules allowed the England player to keep quiet and await the umpire's decision. It came, and it turned out that umpire Aleem Dar hadn't seen the connection of bat and ball (commendably, Dar admitted this). And because Broad declined to walk – to give himself out – he was able to play on. His subsequent haul played a major part in what was ultimately an England victory.

Following the incident, cricket's great and good stepped in to defend Broad, himself a curio among cricketers in being a left-handed batsman and right-arm seam bowler. To a man, they said he had done nothing wrong. He had simply played by the rules, doing the cricket equivalent of a footballer having committed an infringement of the laws of the game – shirt-pulling, say, or tripping an opponent – but playing on until he hears the referee's whistle.

Here's more from Botham: "Stuart Broad did absolutely the right thing in standing his ground". For the former Glamorgan and England player, Steve James, anyone who dared suggest that Broad hadn't covered himself in glory was "sanctimonious". Broad's father, Chris – a former England opener and an International Cricket Council match referee – found the incident amusing. He apparently sent his son a text telling him he had a future in acting.

Time will tell if this is the case, but before we imagine Broad in the role of Ernest and wowing West End theatre audiences let's confine ourselves to the world of sport. In this sphere, Broad's decision not to confess that he'd nicked the ball exemplifies what I believe is an endemic 'ethical dissonance'. (I have deliberately chosen an extreme example, which will doubtless polarise views. Broad did not breach the rules, but his action demands analysis against the higher standard which Jesse Owens exhorted.)

Ethics are present in cricket; they underpin the laws of the game. And yet they're not wholeheartedly embraced. Because of this, ethics end up out of tune. They're dissonant. It's as if we don't understand them.

Let's imagine an alternative scenario for that first test at Trent Bridge. Agar bowls; Broad nicks the ball; it takes a deflection off Haddin and is caught by Clarke. The Australians jump for joy. Soon, though, they realise that the umpire has not given Broad out. It's apparent that Aleem Dar didn't see the connection of bat and ball. Cue frustration. But then cue consternation, when Broad takes off his gloves, turns and walk off the wicket. As he passes Dar, he says: "I clipped the ball. Clarke caught it. I'm out."

What would then have happened? To a man, cricket's great and good would have praised Broad's honesty. They'd have admired him for making a stand. He'd have covered himself in glory and won new fans not just among the England supporters but those supporting the team from Down Under. The venerable Ashes would have been able to boast of a proud sporting moment in which honour, ethical rigour and fair play prevailed over what characterises so much of modern sport: the 'win at all costs, end justifies the means' mentality.

It's not sanctimonious to say that Broad did the wrong thing in not giving himself out. It's not naive and it's not unpatriotic. And perhaps it is not wilfully obscure or fanciful to note that poetic justice later came to bear on the England cricket team, with its dreadful performance in the second Ashes series of 2013 in Australia, a performance that led to a 5-0 humiliation.

Those who argue that Broad was wrong are guilty of one thing only: going against the grain.

But if going against the grain means doing the right thing, something is profoundly wrong with our sporting culture.

The Beautiful Game

Sunday, 6 January 2013. Mansfield Town, a non-league football club, take to the field in a game against Liverpool, one of the most famous clubs in the world.

It's an FA Cup Third Round tie – undoubtedly the biggest game in Mansfield's 2012-13 season. Field Mill, Mansfield's stadium, is packed to the rafters. Everyone who has ever supported the team nicknamed 'The Stags' has got hold of a ticket, eager to see how they fare against their illustrious Premier League opposition.

The first half does not go well for Mansfield. Liverpool's new signing, Daniel Sturridge, scores early on with a well taken goal to mark his Liverpool debut. Liverpool dominate proceedings, elegantly passing the ball as if Mansfield's players have little to do with the game. Liverpool's manager, Brendan Rodgers, would have been entitled to congratulate them at half time, though he may also have cautioned that the home side would up the ante in the second half.

And so it proves. What Paul Cox, Mansfield's manager, said to his players during the interval is not known, but it has a metamorphic effect. His team is transformed. They take the game to Liverpool in an onslaught that must surely lead to a goal. Clearly worried, Rodgers decides, after 10 minutes of relentless pressure, that enough is enough. He brings on Liverpool's far from secret weapon – Luis Suarez, the Uruguayan striker who is as talented as he is controversial. Rodgers had been content to leave Suarez on the bench and rest him for Liverpool's Premier League campaign, but he needs his star player to conjure a response to Mansfield's heroics.

Suarez obliges after just four minutes on the pitch. Liverpool's winger, Stuart Downing, cuts into the penalty box and passes the ball to Suarez. The striker takes it in his stride and shoots on goal, only for his shot to be saved by the Mansfield goalkeeper. However, Suarez follows up his shot with a run directly towards goal. The ball rebounds into his path. And then, in what Diego Maradona might call an act of God but what everyone present would simply say was 'handball', Suarez appears to control the ball with his right hand before smashing it into the net.

He does so nonchalantly, almost indifferently, as if the goal means nothing, as if he knows it will be ruled out.

But Andre Marriner, the referee, allows the goal to stand. It can only be that the experienced official believes this is a case of unintentional handball, an instance of ball to hand rather than hand to ball.

Moments after scoring, Suarez kisses the hand with which he controlled the ball – or, if you like, the hand that was accidentally in the way of the ball. It transpires that he does this whenever he scores as a loving gesture towards his wife and daughter, but neither Mansfield's players nor the club's fans are to know this. In the face of a goal that most football experts later agree should not have been allowed to stand, they perceive insult atop injury. Their discontent is all the more pronounced when the final whistle goes: Liverpool have ultimately prevailed 2-1. Despite a late goal by Mansfield's Matt

Green, their valiant efforts are not enough. Mansfield chief executive Carolyn Radford can only lament that she feels the game "was stolen from us. Whether it was deliberate or not, it should be sorted out."

Afterwards, the media pounce upon Suarez. He is a player with plenty of prior form, and his penchant for controversy had, until his extraordinary feats in the 2013-14 season (when he seemed a player reborn), arguably made for better copy than his football skills. The charge sheet includes his international debut for Uruguay in 2007, when he was sent off for dissent, and another international sending off in the 2010 World Cup quarter-finals, this time for a deliberate handball. He was handed a seven match ban by the Dutch Football Association in 2010 because, while playing for PSV Eindhoven, he bit an opponent, and was also banned by the English FA for eight matches in 2011 for allegedly racially abusing Manchester United's Patrice Evra during a Premier League match. He is often pilloried as a player who dives, an accusation he appeared to mock in October 2012 when he dived in front of former Everton, then Manchester United manager David Moyes, having just scored.

No wonder, perhaps, the instinctive words of ESPN commentator Jon Champion, upon seeing Suarez's goal against Mansfield: "That, I'm afraid, is the work of a cheat". Other journalists, commentators and bloggers were quick to condemn Suarez, though ESPN – perhaps mindful of the threat of a libel action – took the unusual step of apologising for Champion's words.

So far, so typically Suarez. Another game, another goal, another controversy. More column inches. And no doubt, for all that they bemoan his apparently flexible interpretation of the rule book, Britain's football journalists love Suarez as much as they can't get enough of Jose Mourinho, the Special One himself, now reincarnated again at Chelsea as 'The Happy One'. Without figures like Suarez and Mourinho, football isn't so colourful. The back pages are that little bit more prosaic.

Being Professional

But what was most remarkable about the Suarez incident at Mansfield were the comments by former footballers, existing managers and pundits in its aftermath. Virtually all of them agreed that Suarez had no obligation or duty to admit to the referee that he had handled the ball (whether accidentally or not). No less a figure than the hugely respected Gordon Strachan, acting then as a television pundit before going on to become the manager of Scotland, suggested that if Suarez was supposed to confess that his goal was illegal, it would be like expecting people who have got away with parking on double yellow lines to go into council offices and ask to pay a fine.

Liverpool's manager, Brendan Rodgers, also defended Suarez, saying "It's not his job" to own up, and found an ostensibly surprising ally in his counterpart, Paul Cox, who told ESPN, when asked if he felt cheated: "No, I don't. For me to come out and say something like that I think would be quite cheap. If it had gone in the other end and one of our players had done it I think we'd have accepted it." Elsewhere, former Liverpool striker Robbie Fowler said criticism of Suarez was "laughable", adding rhetorically: "If he has to tell the referee that he handled, do the defenders have to go and tell the ref every time they foul a striker?"

Most remarkably of all, the consensus among those in football – save for football writers – was that Suarez had acted professionally. In scoring with his hand, he had simply done what he was entitled to do – to ensure that his team won at all costs, whatever it took. As such, he had been professional. On top of that, the professional thing to do was keep quiet about the handball.

By the end of the 2012-13 football season, Suarez was involved in yet another controversy. It was one that saw him banned by the FA for 10 games. And this time, too – when Suarez clearly bit the arm of an opponent – the word 'professional' could be heard loud and wide. The pundits, commentators, analysts and observers all agreed that this time Suarez really had gone too far. Why? Because biting is bad, yes, but biting the arm of "a fellow professional" (as a footballer turned pundit put it) was incomprehensible. What is truly incomprehensible is the implication behind this comment. It is as if biting among non-professionals goes on all the time, is understood and to be expected. Suarez was this time so beyond the pale because he had done something egregious to a *fellow* professional. It seems, to say the least, that football has an ambiguous relationship with the notion of professionalism.

In this, indeed – the so-called beautiful game (and certainly Britain's most popular spectator sport) – professionalism is equated with dishonesty, either before the event or afterwards. Indeed, ethical dissonance permeates football, so much so that it might be a chant which emanates from the stands, albeit one of more syllables than most. Ethical dissonance saw Liverpool, as a club, not only defend Suarez but desperate to hang onto him in the close season of 2013, when a transfer to Arsenal seemed a serious possibility. It is interesting to note further that Arsenal, a club of tradition and, outwardly at least, one which is more principled than most, were eager to acquire Suarez, knowing full well his dubious track record.

Suarez returned from his ban in the 2013-14 season to hit an extraordinary vein of form, scoring goal after world class goal and helping to propel Liverpool to their best run in the Premier League for years. Playing with a smile on his face, he seemed a man transformed, rid of his demons and a delight to watch. A division down, in the Championship, another of football's modern-day *bête noires* started the season well, only to give his manager an unwelcome early Christmas present thanks to the umpteenth red card of his career. Who else but convicted criminal Joey Barton, sent off – controversially, it should be agreed – in his club Queens Park Rangers' home defeat to Leicester City on 21 December 2013. Barton's career has been so rife with violence that to say it is replete with ethical dissonance would be the understatement of any season.

As football fans, we expect no different of Barton. As fans, we relished the way in which Suarez – so gifted and wonderful a footballer –

seemed to have seen the error of his ways. No wonder Liverpool were desperate to hang on to him – so desperate that the club was reputedly prepared to upend its wages policy to keep him; so desperate that the comments of former Liverpool great, Graeme Souness, to the effect that there was "no way back for Suarez" were forgotten almost as soon as they were uttered.

Until, that is, the FIFA World Cup 2014, held in Brazil, when Suarez inexplicably returned to his bad old ways, biting Italian defender Giorgio Chiellini on the shoulder in an incident which the Uruguayan later said occurred because he "fell" into his opponent. The rest of the world saw things rather differently, including FIFA, which banned Suarez for nine international matches. Italy had salt rubbed into Chiellini's wound: as the Italian players protested to the referee for not penalizing Suárez, Uruguay won a corner. They then scored the only goal of the same, winning 1–0 to qualify for last 16 and sending Italy home.

This time, Liverpool had had enough. Despite Suarez's about turn – he soon admitted that he hadn't fallen onto Chiellini's shoulder and apologised for biting him, vowing that there would never be a repetition of this kind of thing – the Merseyside club sold him to Barcelona on 11 July 2014 in a £75,000,000 transfer. For his part, Chiellini admirably accepted Suarez's apology and indicated that he hoped the whole incident would be forgotten.

It is unlikely that it will be. Suarez is now one of the world's most expensive footballers; his chequered past will be aired time and again. He seems to be an out and out recidivist: a man condemned to repeat his mistakes, to re-enact his crimes sporadically.

Here's hoping, though, that Suarez has finally learnt his lesson. He is a wonderful footballer and it would be a joy to see him play as he did for Liverpool in the 2013-14 season, brilliantly, without incident, within the rules and spirit of the game.

And yet, if we think rigorously about football, Suarez is not as atypical or outlandish as he might at first blush seem. This is world whose elasticity of ethics is inescapable. The same culture that sees clubs turn a blind eye to the worst antics of their star players also explains the professional foul, that which is cynically inflicted but which so many people in football seem to accept is a natural part of its fabric.

Why should it be? Why should we allow the 'Beautiful Game' to have ugliness at its heart? What does it mean for society when the country's most popular game either blatantly, at worst, or tacitly, at best, condones cheating?

This is not to say that the game shouldn't have mavericks and showmen. To look back to the seventies is to behold the likes of Peter Osgood, Alan Hudson, Stan Bowles, Rodney Marsh and Charlie George, not to mention the best of the lot, George Best: brilliant footballers, all, and, by virtue of their cheekiness and inveterate rule-bending, great entertainers. Football fans across the land adored them, and none of them could be said to do things by the book. No one would advocate that footballers should behave like machines, never putting a foot wrong. The game is at once simple, in its aim, but complex in that it is a contact sport with competitiveness at its heart. But the mavericks listed above weren't, by any stretch of the imagination, dirty players. They weren't violent; they weren't the instigators of vicious tackles and foul abuse (though they were not beyond the occasional pre-emptive strike, for example when they knew they would be playing the likes of Norman 'Bites Yer Legs' Hunter and Chelsea's 'Chopper' Harris). What's wrong, in the modern game, is a kind of institutional acceptance of cheating, an attitude that takes it beyond the mischief of the talented maverick and into the realm of concerted, calculated misconduct.

Lance, lies and libel

Tuesday, 15 June, 2004. *The Guardian* runs a story by Clare Cozens about then five-time Tour de France winner, Lance Armstrong. The legendary Texan cyclist is not happy. He is upset about allegations made by *Sunday Times* journalist David Walsh that he took performance-enhancing drugs. Armstrong's lawyers, a well-known London media firm, have set out their client's stall. If there is any repetition of the allegations made by Walsh, in a book which he has co-written with French journalist Pierre Ballester entitled LA Confidential: The Secrets of Lance Armstrong, the result will be a "declaration of legal warfare" by Armstrong.

Indeed, the warfare has already begun. Cozens reports that Armstrong has instructed Schillings to issue libel proceedings in the High Court the following day, the *Sunday Times* having published a story by deputy sports editor Alan English the preceding weekend which roused the cyclist's ire. No wonder, for it was centred on Walsh and Ballester's book. Armstrong plants himself fair and square on the moral high ground: he has never taken drugs, Walsh is the worst imaginable journalist, only English and Ballester can be as bad, the allegations have caused him grave upset, he has shed tears because of them and so have his nearest and dearest. He has no alternative but to go to law.

Fast forward two years, to 2006, by which time Armstrong is a seven-time Tour de France winner. It is reported that Armstrong has settled his libel action – the very same that he brought against Times Newspapers Ltd (the publisher of the *Sunday Times*), Walsh and the deputy Sunday Times sports editor, Alan English, over Walsh's article, which itself referred to the LA Confidential book. As is the form on the settlement of libel actions, the parties agree a statement in open court. It says:

"The *Sunday Times* and Mr Armstrong are pleased to announce that they have settled their legal disputes.

"The *Sunday Times* has confirmed to Mr Armstrong that it never intended to accuse him of being guilty of taking any performance enhancing drugs and sincerely apologised for any such impression.

"Mr Armstrong has always vigorously opposed drugs in sport and appreciates the *Sunday Times's* efforts to also address the problem."

As is also the form, the paper paid damages to the successful claimant. Armstrong pocketed £300,000, and the paper also paid his lawyers' legal costs, which were later estimated to be in the region of £700,000.

There was just one problem with the pleasure both sides took in announcing the cessation of legal warfare. Armstrong was lying through his back teeth. The truth caught up with him some six years later, after he announced his retirement from competitive cycling in February 2011. Armstrong's retirement came at the same time as a US federal investigation into ongoing doping allegations; by June 2012, the United States Anti-Doping Agency (USADA) had charged the illustrious cyclist with having used illicit performance-enhancing drugs. It subsequently announced a lifetime ban from competition on Armstrong and stripped him of each of his Tour de France titles.

USADA's report didn't pull its punches. It concluded that Armstrong had engaged in "the most sophisticated, professionalized and successful doping program that sport has ever seen." It was only a matter of time before cycling's governing body, the Union Cycliste Internationale (UCI), accepted USADA's findings. It duly did so in October 2012. Significantly, Armstrong did not appeal the decision. Just as significantly, though, he continued to deny that he had ever taken performance-enhancing drugs. He clung to the absurdity of his denials until a televised interview with Oprah Winfrey in January 2013.

Billed as a 'no holds barred' interview, Oprah's questions certainly saw Armstrong admit serial wrongdoing and constant lying. It also saw him maintain that he "didn't invent" doping culture, in a mea culpa that also made the point that everyone was at it. Even more poignantly so, too, did Armstrong agree that the mentality underpinning his actions was "win at all costs" – and that he never felt as if he were cheating.

"It was a level playing field," said the man who also confessed that "we [his team] sued so many people I don't even know" [whether they also sued Emma O'Reilly, a whistle-blowing masseuse].

The *Sunday Times* watched the Oprah interview with interest. In a statement, the paper "noted [Armstrong's] numerous admissions regarding taking performance-enhancing drugs. The *Sunday Times* believes that our case for recovering the £1m plus he obtained from us by fraud is now even stronger. We will be pursuing that case vigorously." And so it did, suing Armstrong for the recovery of the compensation paid to him and its legal costs.

Ironically, Armstrong once said of David Walsh: "You know what? They don't even know who David Walsh is. And they never will. And in 20 years, nobody is going to remember him. Nobody." These comments were prefaced by the expression of hope that he, Armstrong, was someone people looked up to.

The ethics of apology

Armstrong was in the wrong. Even he admits this. So why did the *Sunday Times* have to issue legal proceedings to recover wrongly paid damages and legal costs? Why, in summer 2013, was *Cycling News* not able to report that all the monies had been paid back but instead that they were the subject of "ongoing negotiations" (settlement finally occurred later the same year, on terms expressed to be confidential; one hopes that the *Sunday Times* was reimbursed in full)?

In other words, if Armstrong is sorry, why didn't he do the right thing?

What is the status of "everyone" else, sued by the cyclist if they dared, rightly, to question his integrity? Have they been recompensed or are their claims, too, the subject of lawyerly negotiations?

Armstrong is, of course, a vastly different proposition than Suarez or Broad. The errant ways of the footballer and cricketer occurred in the heat of the game or match; Armstrong's cheating was on an unprecedented scale, requiring malice aforethought and the extraordinary nerve and bare-faced hypocrisy to sue those who crossed him. Armstrong's conduct is arguably criminal, in many various ways; this is far from the case with Suarez or Broad. Ethically, Suarez and Broad may be dissonant, but they are still part of the orchestra. Armstrong is a man apart, playing his own unpalatable tunes.

But the trio are united in their privileging of winning over fair play. The end justifies the means; winning is all. And how different could it have been, if Armstrong, at some stage, had stepped forward and truly confessed. If he had had the strength of character to blow the lid on the grandiose methodology of his cheating, how would we now regard him? We might castigate him, yes, but we might also praise him. We might regard the man who saw the error of his ways and came good as better than the man who seems to be engaged in a campaign to convince us that somehow or other he was as much a victim as his legions of admirers. Hence, he feels he has a right to contest the likes of *The Sunday Times* wanting their money back. All's fair in love and war – and sport.

True, but only if everyone abides by the rules. And to show what happens when someone does something different – when a sportsperson bucks the win at all costs, end justifies the means mindset – let's consider the case of Paulo di Canio, the maverick Italian striker who spent seven years in the English Premier League with Sheffield Wednesday, West Ham United and Charlton Athletic.

Di Canio has his detractors. His political views do not appear to be straightforward, and the infamous incident in September 1998 when he pushed referee Paul Alcock to the ground, having been sent off, produced an 11-match ban and equally deserved criticism from football commentators, managers and fans. But in 2000, while playing for West ham, di Canio did something that resulted in him winning the 2001 FIFA Fair Play Award.

In a game against Everton, at Goodison Park, a West Ham player crossed the ball from the right wing. Seconds prior to this the Everton goalkeeper, Paul Gerrard, had collapsed in a heap, having twisted his knee. The ball was heading inexorably to di Canio; just as inexorably, it seemed he would score. Instead, the playmaker and striker caught the ball in both hands. He gestured towards Gerrard and the game was halted for him to receive treatment.

Di Canio received a standing ovation from Everton's fans. Perhaps fittingly, the game ended in a 1-1 draw. What di Canio did was against the laws of the game, but it was for the greater good. No matter that his subsequent career as manager of Sunderland imploded catastrophically. At least, on this occasion, ethics in sport weren't dissonant. They were in tune, and singing from the rafters.

Ethics in sport is not a paradox

Pierre de Courbetin, the founder of the modern Olympics, set the ethical bar for sporting endeavour at the right level when his famous maxim was recorded and played to 100,000 people at the opening ceremony of the 1936 Berlin Olympics: "The most important thing in the Olympic Games is not winning but taking part; the essential thing in life is not conquering but fighting well." We have come a long way from this, so far, indeed, that the following maxims now seem to have more currency than Courbetin's words:

- Nice guys finish last
- Second place is no place
- What's the point of playing, if not to win?
- If you're not first, you're nowhere

The famous American football player and coach, Vince Lombardi, coined a number of similar aphorisms that have sadly come to dominate contemporary sports psychology. Among them are:

- You need fire to win, and there's nothing that stokes a fire like hate
- Show me a good loser, and I'll show you a loser
- If you can accept losing, you can't win
- Winning isn't everything. It's the only thing
- If winning isn't everything, why do they keep score?

Let's step away from Lombardi and remind ourselves of what was in Courbetin's mind when he went about reviving the Olympic Games. Courbetin was a French educator and historian, a man well versed in many things, not least the customs, practices and philosophy of ancient Greece. He was particularly fond of the Athenian idea of the gymnasium, a place which developed and promoted intellectual as well as physical accomplishments. A man of his era (Courbetin was a child of the Franco-Prussian war and, in a sense, a creation of the French Third Republic, that which was formed after the collapse of the Second French Empire, in 1870), Courbetin had a practical use for physical attainment, too. Perhaps because of his country's continued involvement in the war against Prussia (which went on even after France became a Republic), he was a firm believer in the benefits of physical prowess. He saw Thomas Arnold, who pioneered physical education at Rugby School, as a "founder of athletic chivalry", and, into the bargain, regarded him as a man who played a huge part in the success of the British Empire. And pertinently, sport, for Courbetin, was a means of producing first-class warriors.

But if this was so, Courbetin's revival of the Olympic Games stopped well short of the bellicose. He developed a philosophy of sporting competition that was, in many ways, ahead of its time. For example, in promoting amateur sporting endeavour over professionalism, Courbetin nevertheless believed that sportspeople should be remunerated for the time they spent competing, and he fervently rejected the idea that class should play a role in sport, criticising English amateur rowing because it excluded working class competitors. And, harking back to the original Greek games – when a sacred truce was declared among city states and kingdoms for the duration of the games – Courbetin believed that sport had a major role to play in promoting peace.

Courbetin went on to found the International Olympic Committee (IOC) in 1894 and under its auspices the Olympic Games, in the version that has now grown exponentially, were held in Athens in 1896.

Ever since, the Olympics have been prone to controversy (not least with regard to the way in which the IOC has historically operated), but their very controversies illustrate just how deeply sport permeates our lives. It could fairly be said that sport mirrors our moral and ethical selves. Consider the following examples:

- South Africa's policy of apartheid meant it was excluded from the Olympics in 1964. The country's insistence on maintaining apartheid led to life in a sporting wilderness
- 28 African nations boycotted the 1976 Games because the IOC allowed New Zealand to participate; their objection came from New Zealand allowing its rugby team to play in apartheid South Africa
- In 1980, the United States boycotted the Moscow Olympics because the USSR had invaded Afghanistan

Beyond the Olympics, there are numerous other instances of sport being a touchstone for political and socio-cultural issues. Take, for example, the two infamous boxing matches between Joe Louis and Max Schmeling, on 19 June 1936 and 22 June 1938. Louis was a brilliant black American athlete; Schmeling was the pride of Nazi Germany (though he went on to form an enduring friendship with Louis). Schmeling won the first fight, at the Yankee Stadium in New York, knocking out Louis in the 12th round. On the eve of the Second World War, Louis avenged the 1936 defeat, knocking out Schmeling in the first round of the match which was again held at a sold-out Yankee Stadium. Both fights had a racial resonance that far beyond pugilism.

No less significant was Nelson Mandela's action in the 1995 Rugby World Cup, which was held in post-apartheid South Africa. Upon visiting the training camp of the South African team – known as 'the Springboks' – Mandela donned a Springbok cap. He then told the country's players: "The whole nation is behind you." The words and gesture were hugely symbolic given the provenance of the word 'Springbok', which for years was indelibly associated with white, pro-apartheid South Africa. No wonder Mandela's admirable action was much cited for the rest of his life, and that it continues be since his death on 5 December 2013.

In Britain, we have seen the 'Kick it Out' campaign (to rid football of racism), echoed in the Fédération Internationale de Football Association's (FIFA's) prominent anti-racism stance, which was endorsed by a number of star players before each 2014 World Cup game in Brazil. In professional golf, Tiger Woods' extraordinary success has seen him subjected to racist comments (from those who have suggested he is no longer served 'fried chicken' to his former caddy's description of Woods as a "black arse"), all of which have drawn rightful condemnation across the board. Society has moved on from the days of apartheid South Africa and Nazi delight in Schmeling's initial victory against Louis; with it, sport moves on too – and sets the benchmark for what we expect.

Sport, then, is an important ethical barometer. As such, sportspeople have a vital role to play as subliminal educators. Some of them may not like it (not least, some of our present Premier League footballers), but sportspeople are role models. What they do has a major effect on children watching them, and adults, too.

Sport, when its ethics are in tune, is a vehicle for good. We can go further and say that ethical sport is a statement of commitment to human rights. Through sport – sport which is free of ethical dissonance, of cheating and foul play – we learn the value of teamwork, commitment to a greater cause than the self, taking responsibility and discipline. These are vital for the good and harmonious functioning of society. And if sport is played fairly – played ethically – each game leaves a residue far greater than the memory of a good goal, or fine drive, or glorious pass from the baseline.

For Lombardi and his ilk, Shakespeare's words – spoken by King Henry IV in part 1 of the eponymous play – are bang on the money. "Nothing can seem foul to those that win," says the king, before battle. Winning is all; how it happens – whether fairly or not – is irrelevant. But for me, of all the great goals scored by Paulo di Canio, of all the craziness and outlandish controversies, the best thing he ever did was to stop play and pass up a clear goal-scoring opportunity when he saw an injured opponent. That one act by the otherwise unfathomable Italian was unquestionably ethical and *good*.

Or, as Pierre de Courbetin put it: "... the essential thing in life is not conquering but fighting well."

Essay 2: Ethical Entertainment?

"What the mass media offers is not popular art, but entertainment which is intended to be consumed like food, forgotten, and replaced by a new dish." –
W H Auden

The application process for *The Apprentice 2014,* the hit BBC reality TV show which first aired on 16 February, 2005, was underway almost as soon as the 2013 series had been won by an entrepreneurially inclined doctor called Leah Totton. Ms Totton's plans to open a chain of high street Botox clinics, by way of raising standards in the sector, may have provoked consternation among some of the medical profession – who objected to the notion of a 24-year-old and consequently relatively inexperienced doctor bringing cosmetic surgery to the masses – but it's more likely than not that the next round of aspiring *Apprentice* contestants will not share their qualms. Instead, the chances are that they will simply watch reruns of the 2013 show in search of the elusive X-factor-in-business so prised by Lord Sugar, the show's hirer-in-chief, so that they, too, can persuade him to take them on and help make their fortunes.

This is the rationale of *The Apprentice.* The hugely successful show pits a number of young, aspiring businesspeople against each other in a bid to impress Lord Sugar (or his overseas equivalent – the show has been franchised to a number of countries) so much that they are either offered a job or given substantial investment capital. Their only wish is to do right by S'Alun, as he is known in some quarters of the British media; their sole aim in life, it seems, is to be as rich as him or, if this proves impossible (after all, Lord Sugar's net wealth is estimated to be £800m by the authoritative *Sunday Times Rich List),* rather rich, anyway, thank you very much.

For each series, thousands of people do their utmost to be on *The*

Apprentice, itself dubbed "The thinking man's reality TV show" by *The Sun*. They attend auditions up and down the country, at which, according to *Mirror* journalist Julie McCaffrey, the knives are out from the off. McCaffrey posed as a hopeful for the 2007 series, which was ultimately won by Simon Ambrose. She met with ruthlessness and backstabbing among her fellow contenders even as they waited for their turn to be auditioned in a room at the Glasgow Novotel, as McCaffrey revealed, writing in *The Mirror*:

> As soon as one sharp-suited man nips to the loo, his name is called for interview. Quick as a flash, a bloke next to him says: "Sorry, he's gone home. He wants to withdraw his application and told me to tell you."
>
> Everyone suspects he's lying but no one says a word.

This proves to be the standard mode of behaviour for those battling with McCaffrey to make the cut. And things are no better in airings of *The Apprentice* proper. Indeed, writing about the 2007 series, another journalist – Terence Blacker of *The Independent* – did not pull his punches. He said: "The message [the show] conveys every week is that, in order to be a success in business, it is essential to be nasty, disloyal, greedy and selfish."

To view *The Apprentice* today, a full six years on from Blacker's objections, is to see that while the 'prize' may have changed, the show's dubious morality is intact. Where once the winner was awarded a £100,000 a year job as an 'apprentice' to Lord Sugar, today the spoils are an investment of £250,000 in a business of the candidate's creation, with the equity in it split 50/50 with his Lordship. With ratings as high as ever, *The Apprentice* undoubtedly has its allure. It is, to be fair, compulsive viewing. But is it ethical?

In the same way that sport acts as a microcosm of society, from which we learn how to interact and behave, so too does what we regard as successful popular entertainment offer a mirror to our ethical selves. The 2013 series of *The Apprentice* regrettably confirms that ethical dissonance sounds loudly in this sector, too (or, at least, in the way that entertainment culture choses to portray the business world). It may be entertaining, but whether it's ethically edifying is another matter.

The 2014 series will doubtless continue to fly the same unsafe flag but let's take two episodes from series nine, the final of which aired on 17 July, 2013: the first, and the last.

Machetes in the process

Series 1 begins with the familiar dramatic chords of *The Apprentice* soundtrack over which the narrator informs us that "in a harsh economic landscape" there is one man "who has the bottle to take a punt" on entrepreneurs with new business ideas. As the film switches from a bird's eye view of London, S'Alun is that man. We see him leaving the front door of an extremely well-appointed abode and climb into a black limousine whose number-plate is 'AMS 1', a nod not only to Sugar's initials (his full name is Alan Michael Sugar) but also, one imagines, his well-known Amstrad empire. He is sharp-suited and, in a fleeting view of his face as he drives out of the gates of what we assume is his mansion, stern. So he should be, for 16 "ambitious entrepreneurs" are gearing up "to do battle for his backing". The scene, in a just few seconds of deftly directed footage, is set. A battle looms. A battle for the backing of Lord Sugar. A battle which should, by rights, propel the victor towards the kind of wealth accrued by his Lordship.

We then meet the contestants. Their declarations of intent do not lack for self-confidence. Zeeshaan Shah, whom we later learn is the CEO of a property investment company, tells us: "I'm a 'great' of my generation. I'm an innovator and leader of business." As if this isn't bold enough, he adds: "I take inspiration from Napoleon. I am here to conquer."

Next up is Jaz Ampaw-Far, a literacy and education company director. Jaz shares Zeeshaan's self-belief. "I'm half machine," she says. "I can process things at a speed that is out of this world."

If viewers by now discern a theme – of unremitting arrogance, perhaps – they would find it confirmed by the third contestant. Jason Leech is a historian and property entrepreneur who ultimately proves to be one of the more likeable would-be apprentices. That this is so is not evident from his first words: "Some people might come to this process with a game plan. I just feel my effortless superiority will take me all the way."

Aggressive, winner-takes-all pronouncements of brilliance continue in this vein. "I am business perfection personified," says former professional racing driver, Monaco-based Myles Mordaunt. "I have a brain like Einstein," says retail entrepreneur Luisa Zissman, who ultimately comes second (and tells us she has "sex appeal like Jessica Rabbit", though quite why this is relevant remains a mystery). "I will fight to the death to become Lord Sugar's business partner," avows Francesca Macduff-Varley, an ex-ballerina who runs a dance school. The pièce de resistance, though, comes from Neil Clough, who runs regional soccer centres. He sets out his stall in startlingly immoral, perhaps even amoral, terms:

> "I will do anything to win. Cheating, manipulating, I will do it."

Cue the entrance, via a montage, of Lord Sugar. "You've got to be brilliant," he declares. "You've got to get your acts together," he says. "You shut up, and you shut up, and you talk," he orders. "I don't want to see your face anymore," he says. He refers to CVs "full of the usual BS", all of which he is "sick and tired of", for in S'Alun's world "actions speak louder than words". This, after all, is the East End boy who started with nothing and amassed a business empire "worth millions", as the narrator tells us. Failure to please his Lordship results in simple humiliation; the montage closes with Lord Sugar saying, repeatedly, "you're fired" (the show's catchphrase) accompanied by his pointed finger and a look of implacability, as if there could never have been any other outcome.

Once they've been welcomed to the brutal world of business – and given us a brief flavour of their business plans – the candidates have to get on with various tasks over a period of three months. Episode 1 of Series 9 saw them despatched to the port of Tilbury in Essex, where two teams – named, with uncharacteristic modesty and discretion, 'Evolve' and 'Endeavour' – would find a shipping container of imported goods. They then had to sell the goods to "the various trades that open up in this great metropolis of London".

At this point, Sugar's sidekicks are introduced: PR man (and *Countdown* presenter) Nick Hewer, and Karren Brady, a woman who combines any number of roles, from being the vice-chair of West Ham United to small business ambassador to the government, newspaper columnist and author. Brady is one of modern culture's 'media personalities' – eminently capable and talented, seemingly ubiquitous and the winner of any number of awards, largely in recognition of her promotion of women in business. Hewer is no less admired for his business acumen and range of abilities.

What is not so admirable is the way in which *The Apprentice* contestants shape up over the course of three months. The Tilbury task proves tricky for 'half machine' Jaz Ampaw-Far, who elected herself the Evolve team's project manager. She appears to be bossy, disorganised and, worse, unaware of how she is affecting her teammates. Perhaps this utterance, by Jaz in this section of Episode 1, explains why: "I'm only bossy if I'm right – which is a lot of the time. If you're in my way and you're an idiot, you will be moved aside." Jaz previously stated that she "loves being in charge and telling people what to do – it's my idea of heaven." Her leadership proved sorely lacking, and her team failed spectacularly in its task.

The Endeavour team, led by Greek mythology expert Jason, did well. At the time of its victory over Evolve, Jason may have had cause to consider his statements about his brainpower to be vindicated. "My intelligence is like a machete in the jungle," he says, adding to his earlier comment about effortless superiority. "It's just going to take one swipe, and I'll be through." But the trouble with this analogy is that Jason didn't think it through carefully enough. He would later come to find that a jungle is a dangerous place, requiring much more than a single swipe of a machete to survive, but the first victim of Lord Sugar's axe was Jaz. She was fired according to the show's ritualistic formula, dumped out of contention before, as she put it, "I had a chance to show how amazing I am." The experience did not appear to dent her ego: "I really wanted to go right through to the end of the process," says Jaz, "because my business plan is phenomenal."

Interestingly, Jaz is not alone here: various of the candidates, not to mention Lord Sugar himself, refer to the show as a "process". *Der Process* is, of course, the German title of Franz Kafka's great novel of the arbitrary and the absurd in the legal process, *The Trial*, in which the protagonist, Joseph K, is arrested one day without reason and later summarily executed, without ever having been told of his alleged crime. Perhaps the congruence is intentional: Joseph K looks in vain for ethical norms in *The Trial*, and our search is just as fruitless in *The Apprentice*.

Botox on the high street

By the time of the last episode of Series 9 there were just two contenders left: Leah Totton and Luisa Zissman. The rest had been fired, with each sacking providing a vignette in which ethics were at best paradoxically present or, at worst, AWOL.

Take the sacking of Jason, whose machete-like intelligence and effortless superiority did not, ultimately, win the day. Jason was fired in Week 8, by which time he had endeared himself to many viewers by virtue of his fundamental decency. It seems likely that Jason over-egged the grand statements at the outset of the show; certainly, by the time he was made project Manager of Evolve for its task (creating a new online dating concept) in week eight, he was anything but gung-ho and arrogant. In fact, Jason achieved a first in the history of the show, stepping down as project manager at the end of the first day and then working as joint project manager with Luisa.

What happened next encapsulates the values of *The Apprentice*. Evolve, led by Luisa and Jason, decided to target 50-year-olds with their online dating company. Unfortunately, their marketing, design and layout were dreadful. The business would never have been a success but Luisa lost no time in trying to shift the blame for its failure squarely onto Jason's shoulders. Not only did she co-opt fellow contestant Francesca into singing her praises (in return for Luisa doing likewise for Francesca's benefit, in a classic case of mutual back-scratching), Luisa did not pull her punches in condemning Jason, who was undoubtedly guilty of dithering but who some would say acted honourably and fairly in stepping down from being outright project manager in the first place. This decision met with consternation from Lord Sugar, and was the chief reason for Jason's exit. Jason, though, won admirers at this juncture of the show, and not merely because of his juxtaposition with the merciless Luisa (who, said Nick Hewer, "nipped at [Jason's] heels, like a terrier nipping at the heels of a bewildered sheep"). For while his Lordship expressed regret at Jason's departure - "Jason is a very, very nice fella, and I suppose in a way you're sad to see him go. But it was time for him to go" said Sugar – Jason perhaps struck a chord with many when he said, explaining why he ceded the project manager role in favour of Luisa, that he took a "courageous decision", and that "courage comes in many forms". Lord Sugar may have looked on incredulously but there are many people, in all sectors of society, who would be inclined to agree. They might also admire Jason for his disinclination "to go for blood" and possession of a sensibility that, as he puts it, would see him "try to save the women and children first" if he were the captain of a sinking ship (a sentiment that seemed to prompt outright derision from Sugar and Jason's co-contestants).

But self-effacement, discretion, gentility, honourable delegation and allowing others to shine if they have the right skills – these are not qualities espoused by *The Apprentice*. They might be laudable, and they might be a sign of good ethical standards (perhaps, even, simple professionalism), but they are not what the show is about. And nowhere is *The Apprentice's* uneasy relationship with ethics more evident than in the glamorous form of its 2013 winner, Leah Totton (aka 'Dr Totty', as the tabloids, with feminism and equal rights at bay, insisted on calling her). Before we take a look at the prospective arrival of Botox on the high street let's rewind to the penultimate episode of Series 9, the semi-finals in Week 11.

Semi-final stage saw the remaining candidates interviewed by a number of Lord Sugar's trusted associates – Claude Littner, Margaret Mountford, Mike Soutar and Claudine Collins. Sugar says he won't just go into business "with anyone". He needs "the right calibre of person". By now there were five contestants left: Leah Totton, Luisa Zissman, Francesca Macduff-Varley, Neil 'I will do anything' Clough and Jordan Poulton, a business analyst. Jordan, Neil and Francesa were fired, leaving Luisa and Leah to do battle for the £250,000 investment by Lord Sugar. Some remarkable comments and revelations accompanied their departures.

Jordan Poulton, for example, lied about the company behind his business plan. It transpired not only that Jordan did not own the company for which he was seeking investment, but that he proposed to offer Sugar just 15.39 per cent of its equity. Confronted by this, Littner refused to complete the interview with Jordan, labelling him "a parasite", and Sugar fired him unceremoniously, saying he "had nowhere else to go with it". Here, one can only have sympathy with the Amstrad boss. *The Apprentice* makes crystal clear that Sugar's money will only be forthcoming in return for a 50/50 split in a business; moreover, it is obvious that the business plan must be the contestant's, not a third party's. What, we can only wonder, possessed Jordan to chance his arm in this way? Did he gamble that he and his plan would prove so irresistible that Sugar would overlook his blatant lack of transparency? Did he feel comfortable with himself in electing to proceed in this fashion? Or did he, in this world of lax ethical standards and short-cuts, feel that all's fair in love, war and *The Apprentice?*

If so, the show's culture cannot but contribute to the error of Jordan's ways, as distilled by yet another case of ethical dissonance: Neil Clough, the man who said he would do anything, including cheating and manipulating, to win, was fired – but not without Lord Sugar noting that had he been offering a job, rather than investment, as in the early seasons of the show, he would have given Neil "a job tomorrow". Neil – the man "who has been an exceptional candidate" – was fired for inadequacies in his business plan, not for his willingness to cheat and deceive or failings in his moral or ethical sense of the world; meanwhile, Francesca, who, the narrator tells us, "has played fair all the way through" (and who for the most part refused to indulge in games), was also fired – "with regret", it should be pointed out.

And then there were two: Luisa Zissman, with her idea of a website selling to the baking trade, and Leah Totton, with her would-be chain of high street cosmetic surgeons. The two women had wildly divergent business ideas for which they were seeking investment. The press made much of Luisa's plan for wholesale baking utensils being "half-baked", though at least, in its execution, she found it in herself to treat Jason (by now co-opted as one of her team) like a human being rather than an irritating woolly quadraped. Luisa also apologised to the amiable Jason – who by this stage had long since jettisoned his machete, or, perhaps, given it to someone else in the jungle – on comedian Dara O'Brien's wrap-up show featuring the denouement, though whether her contrition came from a sense of genuine remorse or astute PR advice is debateable.

Yet more debateable was Leah Totton's winning business idea: a high-street chain of cosmetic treatment clinics. Notwithstanding Lord Sugar's fear that the cosmetics industry might be "completely alien" to him, he was won over by the Belfast-born doctor, who took part in

The Apprentice while working in the accident and emergency department of a London hospital.

Dr Leah – the name given to Totton's putative high street chain by the Labour peer – was suitably gushing at emerging triumphant: "To have Lord Sugar show this faith in me is absolutely unbelievable," she said. "It's amazing. I had much less experience than the other candidates in business coming into the process and I really can't believe that I have got this far and that I've actually won it. I'm the first person in my family to have even gone to university so it's such a massive achievement for the whole family."

There's that word again: 'process'. And Leah's status as victor of the process was not without some reservations by Sugar himself, let alone the wider world. First, his Lordship changed the name of Totton's business. She had christened it 'NIKS' ('skin' spelt in reverse), despite reservations by her team and, indeed, the public. "It's a bit of a nasty world," Sugar told Leah. "If you can imagine a dartboard and I am the bullseye. This business – it's as if I am leaning out there with my chin waiting to get a smack on it. I am 66 years old. Do I need another load of aggravation?"

Leah's plan would see her sell nine of her clinics for £8m in year-five of Dr Leah's existence as a business, earning Sugar a £3.75m return on his 50 per cent investment. Despite ruminating on the experiences of an "array of friends of a similar age to me … who have had these treatments", Sugar, who has had surgery around his eyes, was persuaded to shelve whatever nascent ethical qualms he might have had by the prospect of "extremely lucrative" returns. "The devil in me is wanting to take a risk," said his Lordship.

'Dr Leah', having opened, complete with skincare range, as suggested by Sugar, will offer a "professional, ethical service" which would offer customers three treatments: anti-wrinkle injections, facial fillers and skin peels. "The profit potential is phenomenal," said Leah. Karren Brady, for one, was convinced by the young doctor, whose manner was rather different to that of the traditional caring medical professional, seeming more like that of the cold-hearted businesswoman. As Brady put it: Leah is an "incredibly bright young woman"… "She really does know what she is talking about. She has shown she can take a gift that she has and use it to create a business. That shows a really unique skill."

There were many who were not quite so enthralled by the young doctor. Dr Leah avowed that she wanted to set up her clinics because she was concerned at the lack of regulation in the cosmetic surgery industry and wanted a safe environment in which women could have facial fillers and skin peels. If we accept this, the 'phenomenal profit potential' is merely a happy side-effect rather than the driving motivation of the business. Trouble is, many people will struggle to buy into Totton's scheme. For all that she insists "I am a very moral person" – and that she'd turn away "young women of 25" who sought Botox – the very existence of her chain creates an ethical conundrum. The industry largely feeds off people's insecurities about their appearance and encourages them not to grow old gracefully but to spend money on artifice. It predicates the superficial above the real, the fake above the natural. And why? So, it seems, that Dr Totton – and Lord Sugar and others – can make money. So that they can take 'Dr Leah' across the pond and 'crack America'.

Ethically, there would seem to be much to cavil about in the very idea of 'Dr Leah'. And ethically, Leah Totton's victory in *The Apprentice 2013* amounts to the perfect summary of the programme's myriad of dubious values. But perhaps the last word should go to a fellow member of the medical profession – an ancient and honourable calling for whom the Hippocratic Oath is sacred:

"[Leah Totton] may have done a few weeks' training in aesthetic medicine, but that is simply not enough," said consultant plastic surgeon Nigel Mercer, a former chairman of the British Association of Aesthetic Plastic Surgeons. "It may not be quite as dangerous as putting a hairdresser in charge of cosmetic surgery, but it is still putting patients at risk."

All of which, remarkably, conspires to make Luisa the more appealing of the two contestants who graced the final of the 2013 series, despite her vicious treatment of Jason, her self-proclaimed identification with Jessica Rabbit as a role model and her self-confessed "hatred" of feminism and for all that she could be described as being a cocktail of contradictions.

All in all it's entertainment, yes. But is it ethical? No one wants a sterile life, full of seriousness and devoid of smiles, but as even this gentle probe of *The Apprentice* reveals, we live in the most curious – ethically speaking – of times.

Essay 3: When Ethics Go AWOL

AWOL: a military term which has entered everyday language in Britain, America, Canada and Australia. It means 'Absent Without Official Leave'. While initially AWOL denoted a soldier who had gone missing without permission, usually with the aim of deserting, it is now used to describe situations in which there has been a radical and unjustified departure from the norm.

If ethical dissonance sounded only in sport and popular entertainment, we could reassure ourselves that all is not rotten in the state of Britain. We might wish that our sportsmen behaved better, and that television executives would commission shows which celebrated honour and morality rather than the survival of the most unscrupulous, but at least we could look beyond leisure and entertainment into the so-called 'real world' and feel heartened by the probity of those in positions of power.

Sadly, British public life is full of incidences where ethics go AWOL. Time and again we are confronted not merely by ambivalence when it comes to ethics but outright corruption. It is as if, for many of those who are privileged enough to have roles in public service, the guiding motto is not 'Do your best to serve the public' but 'Make a fast buck and don't get caught'.

Ethics for officers

On 24 October 2013, *The Times* ran a story with the following headline: "Officers must agree to 'respect and obey law'." Those who gasped in astonishment at the notion that police officers were being asked to agree to respect and obey the law would only have grown more disconcerted by the story itself.

It transpired that in the wake of 'Plebgate' – the infamous incident involving the police, a politician, his bike and an unholy aftermath – the Home Secretary felt it necessary to issue the police with a new code of ethics. Its core message was exactly as per *The Times'* headline – that police officers would be reminded, via the code, of their duty to respect and obey the law. The College of Policing, itself a recent creation of Theresa May (who set it up in 2011 to professionalise the police force), had been tasked with drafting the code. The rationale saw professionalism invoked as the name of the game, with the College writing to its members (serving police officers) and saying it was "professionalising the service in the same way we see the General Medical Council's *Standards and ethics guidance for doctors* or The Bar Council's *Code of Conduct of the Bar of England and Wales*."

In some ways, the announcement that the police were to get their very own ethical charter is not earth-shattering. We live in a world which has a fondness for putting things in writing, for the invention of codes and standards and rules and protocols. We like 'mission statements' and 'what we do' pages on websites. But in another, much more fundamental way, that the police need their own ethical code is deeply worrying; likewise, the fact that it even needs to be enshrined in writing.

In Britain, in living memory, we can invoke the traditional image of the 'bobby on the beat'. He was unquestionably a force for good. He could be stern if he needed to be, but was just as likely to be calming, kindly and helpful. The British constable of the popular imagination was the very embodiment of propriety: a bastion of the community, unerringly law-abiding, respectful of his fellow man and respected, in turn, by all (even criminals).

But just as cutbacks mean that there are now hardly any policemen on the beat anywhere in the country, the standards that the bobby – given televisual realisation in the popular *Dixon of Dock Green* series in the 1970s – represented have also fallen by the wayside. Three episodes over the past three decades illustrate the decline of the police force: the Hillsborough disaster, the death of Stephen Lawrence, and yes, Plebgate too.

To look back at police misconduct on 15 April 1989, the day of the disaster, and afterwards, is to hope and pray the police take to heart any new ethical charter. At Sheffield Wednesday's historic ground 96 fans died in a terrible crush early on in an FA Cup Semi-Final between Liverpool and Nottingham Forest. The crush resulted in injuries to a further 766 people. Those involved ranged from children to the elderly. The tragic incident is Britain's worst-ever stadium-related disaster. What made it all the worse is the behaviour of the police.

Appalling misinformation appeared in the public domain just hours after the disaster. It grew worse and worse, as the police sought to blame fans for what happened rather than take any responsibility themselves. *The Sun* newspaper famously fanned the flames with a front page splash masterminded by its then-editor, Kelvin MacKenzie. MacKenzie's story, headlined 'The Truth', transpired to be wholly inaccurate in blaming the Liverpool fans, and understandably led to *The Sun* being all but boycotted in Liverpool.

But the old saying is that the truth will out – and soon enough it did. The Taylor Report, published in 1990, found that the main reason for the disaster was a failure of police control. As the then Prime Minister, Margaret Thatcher, put it, the "broad thrust" of the Taylor Report amounted to "a devastating criticism of the police." Lord Taylor's inquiry also led to Liverpool's fans receiving their first official exoneration – and to the police being roundly criticised for lying and evasiveness. Later, in September 2012, came the findings of the Hillsborough Independent Panel. This categorically found that no Liverpool fans were responsible for the deaths, and said that attempts had been made by the authorities to conceal what happened, including the alteration by police of 116 statements relating to the disaster.

This figure is extraordinary. It bears repeating: of 164 statements given by police officers, 116 were altered. They were doctored to remove criticism of senior officers and to deflect from the sense of operational chaos that led to the disaster.

How can this ever have been countenanced? How rotten must police culture be to indulge in such a conspiracy of concealment?

Sadly, the answer appears to be "very rotten". Witness the death of Stephen Lawrence, murdered in a racist attack while waiting for a bus on the evening of 22 April 1993. The callous killing of the promising black teenager (Stephen was studying to become an architect) resulted not in justice but in a bungled police investigation, cover-ups and the very racism that animated Lawrence's killers being present in the police. We know this thanks to years of indefatigable campaigning by Stephen's parents, whose efforts led to the then Home Secretary, Jack Straw, announcing that there would be a Judicial Inquiry in July 1997 to be led by Sir William Macpherson.

The Macpherson Report, published on 24 February 1999, found that the police investigation into Stephen's murder was "marred by a combination of professional incompetence, institutional racism and a failure of leadership by senior officers." That is damning enough, but more was to follow. Sir William's focus may have been predominantly on the Metropolitan Police Service (MPS), but he was clear that "institutional racism affects the MPS, and police services elsewhere." In all, he made 70 recommendations aimed at "the elimination of racist prejudice and disadvantage and the demonstration of fairness in all aspects of policing."

Racism is unpalatable wherever it is found. As the Canadian writer Pierre Berton put it: "Racism is a refuge for the ignorant. It seeks to divide and destroy. It is the enemy of freedom, and deserves to be met head on and stamped out." No right-thinking person can argue with this, and no right-thinking person can excuse the culture of police racism that was uncovered by the Macpherson Report. We cannot remind ourselves enough of what Sir William defined as "institutional racism":

The collective failure of an organisation to provide an appropriate and professional service to people because of their colour, culture, or ethnic origin. It can be seen or detected in processes, attitudes and behaviour which amount to discrimination through unwitting prejudice, ignorance, thoughtlessness and racist stereotyping which disadvantage minority ethnic people.

Racism is particularly offensive among the police, however, because of their role and status in society. Police officers are society's upholders of the law. How can they be trusted to uphold the law with regard to racist abuse or assaults, if they themselves are racist?

Ten years on from the Macpherson Report, in April 2009, the House of Commons Home Affairs Committee took evidence from a number of interested parties by way of a stocktake on the extent to which Sir William's recommendations had been implemented. Thankfully, there had been progress – at first blush, indeed, considerable progress, with 67 of Macpherson's recommendations having been implemented. However, problems remained, with black people over-represented in the criminal justice system and discrimination still a problem within the police force. There were a number of "complex factors" for the former, but why, in 2009, had the police not met its target to employ seven per cent of officers from ethnic minority communities? Could it be that racism still exists, inside the institution?

Racism and ethics are poles apart; if the police force is still a place where racism exists, this is less a case of ethical dissonance and more one of an outright wrong. But in the notorious case of Plebgate, I return to the grey and dismaying ground of ethics going AWOL.

This is a tale of allegation, counter-allegation, spin and counter-spin. It starts with a fact: on 19 September 2012, Conservative MP Andrew Mitchell, then the government's Chief Whip, had a row with police officers who would not let him cycle through Downing Street's main gate. This 'fact' was reported in the next day's *Sun* newspaper, with Mitchell accused of having insulted the officers by calling them "plebs". He denied this, but the story refused to blow over and on 25 September a police log of the incident was leaked to *The Daily Telegraph.*

Let's stop here for a minute. We live in a culture which routinely sees leaks of confidential information, especially by politicians but also by the police. If the information being leaked serves to expose iniquity, so much the better. Whistle-blowers should be encouraged to blow the lid on corruption. But too often the leak isn't informed by a noble aim. It takes place to smear an opponent, and/or for financial gain. The former, it seems, was the case with the leak of the police log. Its intention was purely and simply to damage Mitchell.

It worked. By 19 October, with the story continuing to dominate the media, Mitchell had resigned. In his resignation letter to the Prime Minister, David Cameron, he wrote: "The offending comment and the reason for my apology to the police was my parting remark 'I thought you guys were supposed to f***ing help us'. It was obviously wrong of me to use such bad language and I am very sorry about it and grateful to the police officer for accepting my apology."

So, game, set and match to the police, needlessly and basely insulted by the government's Chief Whip? Not quite. On 16 December, a police officer with the diplomatic protection group was arrested on suspicion of misconduct in a public office. Two days later, on 18 December, Channel 4 broadcast CCTV footage which cast doubt on the account of the incident contained in the police log, which claimed that Mitchell's repeated swearing had left members of the public "visibly shocked". The footage suggested otherwise, with only police officers within earshot.

A murky affair was, by now, about clear as mud. A Scotland Yard investigation was launched, with Metropolitan Police Commissioner Bernard Hogan-Howe unconsciously echoing Jonathan Aitken's "shining sword of truth" when he declared: "The allegations in relation to this case are extremely serious. For the avoidance of doubt, I am determined there will be a ruthless search for the truth – no matter where the truth takes us." Operation Alice ensued, and saw the arrest and bail of no less than eight people, five of whom were serving police officers. Plebgate, as it was by now known (the term prevailed over another initial moniker, 'Plodgate'), took yet another foggy path when Mitchell – MP for Sutton Coldfield in the West Midlands – released a transcript of a recording of a meeting he had had at his constituency office on 12 October with Police Federation officers from around the West Midlands. Those officers, in interviews with the media, had claimed that Mitchell refused to give his side of the story and, as such, that he should resign; Mitchell's transcript showed quite the opposite.

It's worth pausing to reflect again here. Mitchell felt he had been the victim, as he put it, of "a stitch-up". He put his money where his mouth was by commencing libel proceedings against *The Sun* and then, on March 31 2013, he lodged a complaint with the Independent Police Complaints Commission (IPCC), accusing the police of engaging in a campaign to destroy his career. But, angered as he was – even potentially right – was it ethical of him to record his meeting with police officers, without telling them? There are many who would say that he was within his rights to do so. There are also those who might say that two wrongs do not make a right.

Plebgate rumbled on. By October 2013, the three officers who had briefed against Mitchell after they met with him a year earlier had issued an apology for their "poor judgement" in speaking to the media. They then appeared before a Home Affairs Select Committee – and said their account of their meeting with Mitchell was "accurate".

By now, the consensus – even among his political adversaries – was that Mitchell was a wronged man. David Cameron stated that his former Chief Whip was owed an apology; so did any number of commentators. In November 2013 the IPCC announced that it would conduct its own investigation into the behaviour of the officers.

What actually happened on that fateful 19 September 2012 day remains unclear. But what is beyond doubt is this: a man lost his job and, from the off, the police behaved in a way that was ethically suspect. The regrettable truth, in British public life, is that they are far from alone.

Politicians on the make

Some time ago – 20 years, in fact – *The Guardian* ran a story alleging that a successful parliamentary lobbyist had bribed two Conservative MPs. The lobbyist was Ian Greer, of Ian Greer Associates. The MPs were Neil Hamilton and Tim Smith. They were accused of asking parliamentary questions on behalf of Mohamed Al-Fayed, the owner of Harrods.

Al-Fayed told the much-respected political journalist David Hencke, whose story appeared in *The Guardian* on 20 October 1994:

"I was approached by Ian Greer, who offered to run a campaign. He came to me at my home and offered his services. You must remember that at the time we were in a desperate situation, facing a barrage of criticism from MPs run by Tiny Rowland like Edward Du Cann.

"He told me he could deliver, but I would need to pay. A fee of about £50,000 was mentioned. But then he said he would have to pay the MPs, Neil Hamilton and Tim Smith, who would ask the questions.

"Mr Greer said to me: 'You need to rent an MP just like you rent a London taxi.'

"I couldn't believe that in Britain, where Parliament has such a big reputation, you had to pay MPs. I was shattered by it. I asked how much and he said it would be £2,000 a question."

Messrs Greer and Hamilton denied the allegations. Smith admitted accepting payments (albeit from Al-Fayed directly, not Greer) and resigned. Libel suits were brought and, for months, the front pages of the UK press were dominated by the story. The Prime Minister at the time, John Major, set up the Nolan Committee to review standards in British public life. Eventually, confronted by the weight of damning evidence against them, Hamilton and Greer withdrew their libel actions. Their downfall continued with Greer's company collapsing and Hamilton declaring bankruptcy. Hamilton also lost his seat as Conservative MP for Tatton, Cheshire, roundly defeated by former BBC reporter Martin Bell. Despite his fall from grace, Hamilton went on to reinvent himself as something of a media personality (once describing himself, during a celebrity edition of *Mastermind*, as "an object of professional curiosity") and even, in 2011, sowing the seeds for a revival of his political career by being elected to UKIP's National Executive Committee.

What became known as the 'Cash for Questions' scandal took in a number of other players – not to mention additional legal proceedings, when Hamilton sued (unsuccessfully) Al-Fayed for libel. But perhaps its most significant legacy was the creation of the Committee on Standards in Public Life, which was a consequence of the Nolan Committee.

The Nolan Committee, whose formation John Major announced in the House of Commons on 25 October 1994, had clear original terms of reference, viz.:

> To examine current concerns about standards of conduct of all holders of public office, including arrangements relating to financial and commercial activities, and make recommendations as to any changes in present arrangements which might be required to ensure the highest standards of propriety in public life.

The Committee got to work in earnest, and soon enough declared (in its first Report, dated 11 May 1995) Seven Principles of Public Life as "a re-statement of the general principles of conduct underpinning public life." The Principles, which continue to define the Committee's work, are:

- **Selflessness** – Holders of public office should act solely in terms of the public interest. They should not do so in order to gain financial or other benefits for themselves, their family or their friends.
- **Integrity** – Holders of public office should not place themselves under any financial or other obligation to outside individuals or organisations that might seek to influence them in the performance of their official duties.
- **Objectivity** – In carrying out public business, including making public appointments, awarding contracts, or recommending individuals for rewards and benefits, holders of public office should make choices on merit.
- **Accountability** – Holders of public office are accountable for their decisions and actions to the public and must submit themselves to whatever scrutiny is appropriate to their office.
- **Openness** – Holders of public office should be as open as possible about all the decisions and actions they take. They should give reasons for their decisions and restrict information only when the wider public interest clearly demands.
- **Honesty** – Holders of public office have a duty to declare any private interests relating to their public duties and to take steps to resolve any conflicts arising in a way that protects the public interest.
- **Leadership** – Holders of public office should promote and support these principles by leadership and example.

Interestingly, when first articulating what are known as the 'Nolan Principles', the Committee did not excoriate those whose conduct had prompted its creation. Instead, by way of what a cynic might say was a whitewash, the First Report stated that "it was not possible to say conclusively that standards of behaviour in public life had declined." However, the First Report conceded that "it was possible to say that conduct in public life was more rigorously scrutinised than in the past, that standards demanded by the public remained high, and that the great majority of people in public life met those standards." In light of these substantial caveats, the Report noted "weaknesses in the procedures for maintaining and enforcing those standards, which meant that people in public life were not always as clear as they should have been about where the boundaries of acceptable conduct lay."

In other words – perhaps those of the man on the Clapham omnibus, world-weary and expecting nothing from British politicians – there was a lot more attention on people in public office, thanks to the ever-prying media, so it would pay to be careful and remember how to behave well.

To jump from the dying embers of political life in the late 20th century to the brave new world of early 21st century politics is to find the Committee on Standards in Public Life still there, beavering away on Horse Guards Parade in the heart of London, reporting as an independent advisory body to the government of the day and maintaining what its website calls "a constant presence." It is also, sadly, to find that there are many in public life who act as if they have never even heard of the Seven Principles, still less thought about living and working in accordance with them.

Time and again a scandal breaks in which the same nexus of overarching greed and ethical impropriety, not to say outright corruption, emerges as the guiding principle of a public officer's conduct. Here are just a few examples in which, just as in Plebgate and the original Cash for Questions debacle in the mid-1990s, ethics have gone AWOL:

- Cash for Honours. To be a peer of the realm in Britain is an honour afforded only to a very few. Once upon a time hereditary peerages were the sole preserve of the ruling aristocracy, but the Life Peerages Act 1958 changed this elitist practice so that life peerages could be granted to a wide range of deserving individuals.

The prestige, though, seem to be just too tempting for some, who seek to attain such glory by fair means or foul – whatever it takes, for the end justifies the means. In the latter category, it emerged, in 2006 and 2007, that various men nominated for life peerages by then Prime Minister Tony Blair had coincidentally loaned large amounts of money to the Labour Party. No criminal charges were ever brought but the Labour Party repaid the donations. "We've got to stop this perception that parties can somehow be bought by big donations either from very rich people, or trade unions, or businesses," opined David Cameron.

Quite – and yet Cameron went on to find himself at the centre of a cash-for-peerages row following the appointment of two wealthy Tory backers to the House of Lords. Financier and party co-treasurer Michael Farmer and businessman Ranbir Suri were among 12 new Conservative working peers announced by the Prime Minister in August 2014. It transpired that both have made donations to the Conservative party, according to analysis by the Electoral Reform Society (ERS). Mr Farmer donated more than £6.5 million, while Mr Singh, a former general secretary of the Board of British Sikhs, donated £312,435 – either personally or through his company Oceanic Jewellers. The words of ERS chief executive Katie Ghose are to the point: "These appointments further cement the impression that to get into the House of Lords, all you have to do is write a fat cheque to a political party or be a party hack," she said.

- MPs' Expenses. Let's look back to 2009. Here we saw a scandal that defied belief. We owe our knowledge of the MPs' expenses scandal to the *Daily Telegraph,* which, in May and June 2009, published a series of revelations of outright fraud and corruption on behalf of a number of MPs.

Andrew Pierce, then the assistant editor of the *Telegraph*, later revealed that his paper had paid £110,000 for information about MPs' expenses. He said it was "money well spent in the public interest". It is very difficult to argue with this view, given what was uncovered by the *Telegraph*.

An extraordinary number of areas of abuse were uncovered, albeit that, rather curiously, Tony Blair's expenses were inadvertently shredded ("by mistake", said his office) upon receipt of a Freedom of Information Act request for sight of them. It is worth noting, by the way, that there were a number of legal proceedings arising from Freedom of Information Act requests for disclosure of MPs' expenses before the story broke. MPs – those who ratified the passing of the Act in 2000 – did their level best to evade its provisions. Ultimately the *Telegraph's* decision to publish and be damned was right, making a nullity of their desperate scrabbling around, which included Harriet Harman, then the Leader of the House of Commons, tabling a motion that would make the disclosure of MPs' expenses exempt from the provisions of the Freedom of Information Act.

Needless to say, our avaricious MPs didn't stop there. They over-claimed for food, for travel, for council tax. They sought money that wasn't due to them for furnishing their homes and living in 'grace and favour' homes. They exploited the 'no receipt' rule, submitting swathes of claims each under £250 – for which they weren't obliged to produce receipts. They did all this, and more, and they were all at it: Conservatives,

Labour, Peers – parliament's shamelessness knew no bounds.

For the *Times,* the scandal was "Parliament's darkest day". It led to criminal charges (and sentences), to resignations, to suspensions from the House of Lords, to falls from grace and to the creation of the Independent Parliamentary Standards Authority, this to manage at arm's length (from the House of Commons) the business of MPs' expenses. Yes: the scandal ended the MPs' time-honoured ability to deal with their own expenses. And, like Plebgate and the consequential need for the police to be reminded of the law, it revealed that something wasn't just rotten in the state of Denmark.

- The embodiment of what was wrong in Denmark is perhaps the behaviour of Lord Jack Cunningham – 'Junket Jack', as he is has been labelled. The Labour MP for Copeland between 1983 and 2005 served in Tony Blair's cabinet before becoming a life peer. His career has been dogged by controversy: when serving as Minister for Agriculture, he displaying a flexible notion of socialism by chartering seven private chartered flights in just 13 months (at a cost to the taxpayer of £45,000). Having become agriculture minister, Cunningham lost no time in sprucing up his office, reportedly spending £2.3million in moving from Whitehall to Smith Square. This move entailed the acquisition of a mahogany desk which cost over £10,000; later Cunningham was to opt to fly to a conference in America by Concorde instead of taking a cheaper flight, this costing £3,452. He also decreed that fresh flowers had to be delivered to his office – daily, from Kew Gardens. Finally, in 2013, he was suspended as a peer when he became embroiled in a scandal, having allegedly sought £144,000 a year for lobbying services. Undercover reporters from the *Sunday Times* maintain that Cunningham promised to exert his influence for cash, apparently telling reporters posing as representatives of a South Korean solar energy company that "Knocking on doors, introductions and getting to see the people, including if necessary the ministers – this is part of the package." For his part, Cunningham says that he knew the reporters were fake, and that he was 'testing' them. Time will tell – along with other Lords, Cunningham is being investigated by the House of Lords commissioner for standards – but cash for influence has sadly been definitely seen elsewhere...

- Cash for Influence. What to do if you're an MP and a lobbying company contacts you, to offer fees of £3,000 to £5,000 per day to represent its clients' interests in return for money? The correct answer, for an MP familiar with the Nolan Principles and basic precepts of sound ethical conduct, is to run a mile. But in 2010, even as the expenses scandal raged, a number of MPs demonstrated that when it comes to making a fast buck, their scruples are few and far between. This time it wasn't the *Daily Telegraph* but the *Sunday Times* which broke the story of yet more disgraceful conduct among MPs, setting up a fictitious lobbying enterprise and tape-recording interviews with various MPs. The egregiousness of the latter was startling.

Margaret Moran, former Labour MP for Luton South, accomplished a double whammy: not only was she found guilty, at Southwark Crown Court, of expenses' fraud, she also claimed to be able to call upon a "girl's gang" to help the bogus company's (thankfully non-existent) clients.

Stephen Byers, a man who occupied high office in the Labour government (and who survived other controversies), said that he had previously influenced government policy for cash. Only too happy to accept the proposed fee of up to £5,000 a day, he echoed Ian Greer and the Cash for Questions scandal of some 20 years earlier, a scandal that Byers would have been only too aware: I'm "sort of like a cab for hire", said Byers.

Geoff Hoon, like Byers one of the UK's most senior politicians, declared that he was keen to "make money" out of his contacts and knowledge.

Hoon and Byers were banned from parliament; Hoon for five years, Byers for two.

The state of Denmark: ethics are AWOL and expertise is for hire

These are among the headline-grabbing stories that show that things aren't just rotten, they're arguably beyond repair. How is it possible that MPs have learnt nothing from the Cash for Questions scandal? How can they so casually disregard the Nolan Principles? Are there any honest MPs, or is everyone on the make, and just the unlucky found out? And can we blame huge numbers of British people for their apathy about politicians and cynicism about their motives and promises?

In truth, endemic apathy is to be expected. Our politicians get the electorate they deserve: an oft-despairing one, and, increasingly, one which simply expects its public officers to behave badly. Confronted by the latest scandal, we shrug our shoulders and shake our heads but though we may be outraged we're no longer horrified.

We've got used to it. We've got used to ethics being AWOL and cabs being piloted by chancers instead of those who've spent the three to five years that it takes to learn The Knowledge, without which a cabbie won't get a licence to drive one of London's black cabs.

It's as if everyone has their price.

And it's as if everything has its price – from judicial policy (witness the present government's onslaught on legal aid and access to justice, one which makes a nullity of cherished, fundamental principles like the rule of law and the availability of justice for all; so too its attempts to curtail the availability of the judicial review mechanism) to medical policy (it wasn't until late 2013 that GlaxoSmithKline, for example, announced that it would end its practice of paying doctors to prescribe and promote its drugs). Into the bargain come bankers and banking, insurers and the insurance industry; cosy cousins are the worlds of sport and entertainment.

And then, reporting on all this, keeping a watchful eye, keeping tabs, taking seriously its role as the guardian of our collective moral fibre, is the media. A number of legal reasons arising from the phone-hacking trials prevent me from discussing the extent to which ethics are AWOL in the media. Allow me simply to cite William Bernbach, an American advertising executive, who said: "All of us who professionally use the mass media are the shapers of society. We can vulgarize that society. We can brutalize it. Or we can help lift it onto a higher level."

I hope, as a consequence of the Leveson Inquiry and whatever might be the outcome of the phone hacking trials (despite some guilty pleas and findings, retrials and initial trials of other suspects are pending), that things like the hacking of Milly Dowler's phone – prohibited by existing laws, which journalists chose to ignore – will never happen again. I hope that all involved in the Fourth Estate will work to lift it onto a higher level. Meantime, I will turn my attention to the world of big business.

Here, too, things are awry.

Essay 4: Big Business, Bad Ethics

All for ourselves, and nothing for other people, seems, in every age of the world, to have been the vile maxim of the masters of mankind – Adam Smith

The world has moved on since Adam Smith published *The Wealth of Nations* in 1776. Smith's work remains a classical treatise of economics and the factors that create wealth, but in his day – when distinctly unethical practices such as the slave trade and colonialism were at their height – the notion of Corporate Social Responsibility (CSR) was unknown.

Today, things are very different. Big businesses around the world have accepted that they need to have sound ethical policies – that they need to behave ethically, and that they need to be seen to be ethical. The sea change arguably began as the Cold War ended, with the term 'business ethics' gaining currency in the United States in the 1970s. There, 1980 saw the formation of the Society for Business Ethics, an international organisation whose purpose is simple: 'We're here to keep people talking about business ethics', says the Society. The notion of business ethics spread across the Atlantic, and further afield, so that now it is a rare corporation indeed that does not have a CSR policy.

And yet, for all that CSR – commuted by many organisations simply to Corporate Responsibility (CR), as if to widen its scope – is prevalent as a business buzzword, sometimes its embrace is merely notional. Sometimes it's a part of a company's make-up for a simple reason: competitive advantage, something cynically hi-jacked for appearances' sake. And other times it is flagrantly disregarded, as if, sadly, we live in a world which is no different to that which prompted Adam Smith's observation about "the vile maxim of the masters of mankind".

When big business behaves badly

Big business scandals occur with dismaying frequency. Here is an inglorious Top Five instances of big business behaving badly in the past few years.

1. Savar Factory Collapse in Bangladesh

In April 2013, 1,135 people were killed in an accident that was entirely preventable. The eight-storey Rana Plaza, a factory complex in the district of Savar on the outskirts of Dhaka (the capital of Bangladesh), collapsed, killing thousands and injuring a further 2,515 people. Intense scrutiny by the worldwide media in the days following the tragedy revealed that the building's owner had sidestepped building regulations: the upper floor had been built without a permit, and was in any event intended to be used for shops and offices, not factories with heavy machinery. Moreover, the owner had ignored a number of warnings that the large complex (which housed a total of 5,000 people working in different roles) was unsafe, ordering garment workers to return to work on the day of the disaster despite warnings the preceding day that large cracks had appeared in the building. Experts subsequently revealed many other breaches of basic construction norms.

Bangladesh is the second-largest exporter of clothing behind China. A number of large Western companies in the fashion trade source clothing from the country. It is extremely cost-effective to do so, given the extraordinarily cheap labour there (Bangladesh has the lowest minimum wage in the world – a mere $37 a month).

In the wake of the Savar building collapse, Western retailers banded together to sign up to a plan that requires them to help finance fire safety and building improvements in the factories they use in Bangladesh. The goal would be the creation of "a safe and sustainable garment industry in Bangladesh... in which no worker needs to fear fires, building collapses or other accidents that could be prevented with reasonable health and safety measures."

A good initiative but, as the *New York Times* put it in an article dated 13 May 2013, Bangladesh's "low wages and lack of regulation have helped it attract billions of dollars in orders from Western retailers and apparel brands."

Which begs two questions. One, could it be that colonialism lives on, in an altogether more exploitative and insidious fashion than its guise in Adam Smith's era? And secondly, why did it take such a terrible event to force Western retailers to do better? The likelihood is that if the Savar building had not collapsed, big business would have carried on, regardless – the defence being that companies exist to maximise shareholder returns. True enough, but at what cost?

2. McDonald's – not lovin' it all that much

The United States is not alone in having a love-hate relationship with unions. Many countries ideologically applaud the existence of unions, only to find them, well, a bit of a pain. Perhaps this is because they have a habit of giving their members a voice, and alerting them to their rights.

McDonald's, the world's leading purveyor of fast food (which, I think many of us will admit, we've enjoyed once in a while, even if we haven't been to that many of its 36,000 restaurants in 119 countries), doesn't like unions. At all. It has perennially refused to acknowledge any attempts by employees to band together and form a union, using the might of the law to do so. Hardy workers in McDonald's in St Hubert, Quebec, Canada, did their best to buck the trend, with many of them signing up to a collective bargaining agreement in 1997. McDonald's didn't like this. When a variety of ways to scupper the embryonic union failed, the corporation took the draconian step of closing the St Hubert franchise. "None of us is as good as all of us," goes a McDonald's slogan, in franchises around the world – but if the all get too big for their boots, it seems that they might as well become the none.

Indeed, the history of McDonald's is so rife with dubious ethical practices and decisions that it is a wonder we continue to love it – as the slogan goes – quite as much as we do. Perhaps modern society has become too keen on instant gratification to worry about ethical implications, but if we cast our minds back to the infamous McLibel case it might, perhaps, be enough to warrant a fresh look at our seemingly unthinking delight in Big Macs.

McLibel was one of the single biggest PR disasters of all time. McDonald's decided to sue Helen Steel and Dave Morris for libel under the laws of England and Wales, the pair having been instrumental in distributing leaflets which promised to reveal 'the truth' about McDonald's practices. The leaflets bore words like 'McDollars', 'McGreedy', 'McCancer', 'McMurder', 'McProfits' and 'McGarbage'; Steel and Morris also distributed material saying: 'What's Wrong with McDonald's? Everything they don't want you to know.' They alleged that McDonald's was engaging in "promoting Third World poverty, selling unhealthy food, exploiting workers and children, torturing animals, and destroying the Amazon rainforest," too.

Far-fetched? To a degree: when what became the longest ever trial in an English court (it lasted for two and a half years) was finally over, the court held that Steel and Morris had not proved all of their allegations. But victory for McDonald's was pyrrhic: an award of £60,000 in damages, which Steel and Morris promptly refused to pay. By this stage, sense was prevailing among those at the top of the food-chain at McDonald's: they elected not to try and enforce the award. Later, the Court of Appeal ruled that it was fair comment to say that McDonald's employees worldwide "do badly in terms of pay and conditions", and true that "if one eats enough McDonald's food, one's diet may well become high in fat... with the very real risk of heart disease."

Later, in 2001, came the polemical *Fast Food Nation: The Dark Side of the All-American Meal* by Eric Schlosser (made into a Richard Linklater-directed film starring Ethan Hawke and Bruce Willis in 2006) and the even more damning *Super Size Me* in 2004, Morgan Spurlock's evisceration of McDonald's at the expense of his own health. From 1 February to 2 March, 2003, Spurlock ate only McDonald's food, to test the company's claims that it is healthy and nutritious. Spurlock's physical and mental health as a result of eating McDonald's for breakfast, lunch and dinner deteriorated badly, and it took him 14 months to lose the weight gained during his experiment.

Critics say that Spurlock simply revealed what we all know: that fast food is not healthy food. True enough. But is it ethical to pay workers low wages, foil their attempts to unionise and sue critics? Or does an early instance of McDonald's founder Ray Kroc's behaviour distil an unethical essence at the heart of the company? In 1972, Kroc donated $250,000 to Richard Nixon's re-election campaign. By way of a happy coincidence, 'the McDonald's bill' was then on the US statute books. This would allow employers to pay their teenage employees 20% less than the federally-mandated minimum wage. They weren't exactly getting much even at the minimum wage – then $1.60. Taking them down to $1.28 an hour wasn't greeted with joy.

3. Pay day loans – ethical usury?

Cometh the global financial downturn, cometh the pay day loan companies. Initially taking root in the United States, pay day loan companies have grown rapidly in the UK over the past five years. A sorry sight in many high streets in Britain's poorer areas are not the small, independent retailers that once managed to make a living but their replacements: gaudy businesses which promise – and deliver – 'instant cash', on the basis that the borrower will repay it on his or her pay day. ('Fast cash for fast lives', was one company's advertising slogan.)

Pay day loan companies test to the limit the famous English legal commentator William Blackstone's dictum about interest versus usury: "When money is lent on a contract to receive not only the principal sum again, but also an increase by way of compensation for the use, the increase is called *interest* by those who *think* it lawful, and *usury* by those who do not", wrote Blackstone, in his *Commentaries on the Laws of England.*

Usury, of course, is a popular theme in religious writing and literature. Shakespeare gave us Shylock in *The Merchant of Venice*; Balzac's eponymous character in his 1830 novel *Gobseck* was no less fond of money-lending. The Bible is replete with references (of varying import) about money-lending; charging interest is prohibited under Islam. The Roman statesman and philosopher Cato summed up the view of many thinkers when he said: "What do you think of usury? – What do you think of murder?"

But for all that usury – the practice of making unethical or immoral monetary loans, i.e. those with exorbitant rates of interest – has been condemned throughout history, the pay day loan sector is in rude health. In the UK, the average pay day loan costs up to £25 for every £100 borrowed; there is no restriction on rolling over loans, meaning that it is only a matter of time before a person taking a pay day loan has run up a huge debt (one certainly not repayable on a pay day – unless it's via a lottery win). It is estimated that, in 2009, 1.2 million people took out 4.1 million loans, with total lending amounting to £1.2 billion. One shudders to think of how many people now, five years later, are caught up in the pay day loan spiral of astonishing APR of anything between 1,000% and 2,000%.

The Archbishop of Canterbury, Justin Welby, publicly criticised pay day loan companies in 2012 (when he was the Bishop of Durham), calling one operator's high interest rates "shocking and "usurious". The Rev Welby reiterated his criticism in 2013, though at this point he said he wanted to see competition, rather than legislation, put the sword to the pay day loan sector. Political and media criticism of the pay day loan companies has been widespread, perhaps most notably from the Labour Party leader Ed Miliband in November 2013. Miliband condemned the pay day lenders for creating "a quiet crisis of thousands of families trapped in unpayable debt." He also called for cartoon-type ads by pay day operators aired during children's programmes to be banned, and promised to introduce legislation to that effect.

And yet, for all the deserved criticism, nothing has changed. The pay day loan companies continue to take advantage of those who are desperate and needy, promising them an instant fix before trapping them in a spiral of terrible, unrelenting debt. Usury has never been ethical; in the modern world, under the pay day loan companies, it is nothing short of a disgrace.

4. Ryanair and the pledge to be nice to customers

Low-cost airline Ryanair has become a byword for abysmal customer service (something of a shame given its leading role in making air travel more affordable), topping a *Which?* poll in 2013 for the worst customer service out of Britain's 200 biggest brands. The magazine asked consumers to rate each company according to its staff's knowledge, attitude and ability to deal with issues. Ryanair scored two stars (out of a possible five) for each category, producing an overall rating of 54 per cent. This was easily the lowest of the 100 companies, but it was hardly a surprise: the airline's boss, the combative Michael O'Leary, seems to have been on a mission to alienate people ever since took the helm of the company in January 1994.

O'Leary has a radical view of the notion that 'the customer is always right'. Here's what he once said: "People say the customer is always right, but you know what – they're not. Sometimes they are wrong and they need to be told so." Another notorious Ryanair declaration was on refunds: "You're not getting a refund so **** off. We don't want to hear your sob stories. What part of 'no refund' don't you understand?"

A list of the controversies surrounding Ryanair would be enough for a book in its own right; there is, in fact, a blog dedicated to the failings of the no frills airline called I Hate Ryanair (http://www.ihateryanair.org). Like McDonald's, Ryanair doesn't like its employees forming unions; the airline's online check-in system seems geared to catch out the unwary, who are charged extra if they fail to arrive at an airport without online forms which they are supposed to print out; its "cavalier treatment of passengers" (as described by *The Economist*) is legendary; its advertising campaigns are often as misleading as they are offensive.

But it seems that Ryanair is going to reform its image. It was announced, in February 2014, that the airline would become more 'touchy feely', and that it would introduce allocated seating instead of allowing the habitual stampede among customers for seats. O'Leary, it seems, would be stepping out of the limelight, albeit that press statements released by the airline insisted that he would still be as involved as ever.

Those same press statements praised O'Leary for being "great PR" over the past 20 years. That same PR, before the seeds of Ryanair's rebrand, saw the airline dismiss the results of the *Which?* survey as "useless" – a "survey of 3,300 people, including their pet hamsters, gerbils and goldfish."

Ryanair, historically, has presented us with a brash disregard for anything resembling ethical conduct. The adage of doing unto others as one would have done to oneself seems to have been nowhere in its thinking. All that appears to have mattered is profit: O'Leary himself is one of Ireland's wealthiest men. It is to be hoped that the airline's new modus operandi is not simply a cynical branding exercise but is in fact motivated by a sense that ethics do, after all, have a place in business.

5. Citigroup – the $50m private jet (that never was)

In 2008, the US government had to step in to rescue Citigroup as the subprime mortgage crisis began to tear apart what was once the world's biggest bank. Several major financial institutions, such as Lehman Brothers, Fannie Mae, Freddie Mac and American International Group (AIG), had already either gone under or been bailed out; the 2008 AIG bailout was the largest government bailout of a private company in US history. The Citigroup bailout was part of the government's Troubled Asset Relief Program (TARP) initiative, which President Bush authorised and made law on 3 October, 2008. TARP enabled the government to purchase assets (often collateralized debt) and equity from troubled financial institutions, the aim being to create liquidity and stop the financial crisis of 2007-08 from getting any worse.

"This is a tough situation for America, but we'll recover from it," said President Bush as his government rode to the rescue of Citigroup. "The first step for recovery is to safeguard out financial system."

It is worth remembering how the world greeted the 2008 crisis. It is no exaggeration to say that it seemed as if life as we know it was about to collapse. Everything that so many of us had taken for granted – and accepted as certainties – seemed to have been trampled into the ground, by a blend of greed, arrogance and ignorance. This book is not the place for forensic economic or financial analysis, and in the interests of making my point I will say simply this: the effects of what happened in 2008 are still being felt today, even as the Citigroup bailout led to the bank once again being in rude health, with the bank having $420 billion in surplus liquid cash and government securities as of June 2012.

And my chief point is this: from what planet did the notion of upgrading to a new $50 million, twelve-seat corporate jet – despite being in receipt of a government bailout of $45m – come from? How was this idea ever signed off? How could it possibly have been seen as ethically acceptable?

This is what Citigroup decided to do, in January 2009. It wasn't even as if the financial crisis had been well and truly reversed. The American public – and the world at large – was still smarting from the disastrous previous year.

And yet Citigroup felt it reasonable to invest in a new plane, the Dassault Falcon 7X, a luxurious jet with, as the *New York Post* put it, "plush interior with leather seats, sofas and a customizable entertainment center."

Outcry led to the cancellation of the agreement to acquire the jet. A spokesman soon confirmed that there was "no intent to take delivery of the new aircraft." There would be, though, a penalty for breach of contract, with CNN reporting that the penalty was likely to be between $3 and $4m.

Sound ethical thinking in the first place would have avoided both public outrage, and a financial penalty for breach of contract.

Business knows what's best – and what's right

In each of my inglorious five, there is a common denominator: money. Or rather, *greed* for money. To the question, 'how much is enough?', the answer seems to be, 'too much is never enough'. Always needing more than enough means that the most basic ethical precepts are ignored or forgotten – assuming they were ever known in the first place.

Philosophers, wearing a devil's advocate hat, might be tempted to note that corporations may be legal entities, so far as the law is concerned, but that they are nevertheless *abstractions* of human enterprise, 'machines', as it were, with a will and minds of their own. Those minds, as corporate minds, by definition can't understand ethics or know they exist. But lawyers are familiar with an expression by which the court can go behind the inhuman corporation: it is 'piercing the corporate veil'. By so doing, we find that even a vast behemoth, such as McDonald's, is run by human beings. Even the biggest company, then, knows the difference between right and wrong – and knows that ethics exist.

Abstractions aren't good enough. They need to be put aside. Big business needs to be better – and big business needs to embrace ethical propriety not as a cynical means of securing competitive advantage but because to do so is *right*.

Ethically, bankers' bonuses present something that is less of a conundrum and more in the nature of another dismaying example of big business simply not having its house in order. And here, there is no need to peer behind the corporate veil. The recipients of bonuses are human beings; the decisions to award them are made by their fellow human beings.

Take, for example, the Royal Bank of Scotland – bailed out by UK taxpayers during the financial crash of 2008-2009 with a £45bn investment – and its plans, announced in early 2014, to pay £588m in staff bonuses. This was despite suffering an £8.24bn loss in 2013.

RBS's CEO, Ross McEwan, was on the money when he acknowledged that the issue of paying bonuses was "highly emotional". But he made the standard justification, that which the City is always ready to trot out – that if such bonuses weren't forthcoming, the bank wouldn't have the right people in the job. "I need to pay these people fairly in the marketplace to do the job," said McEwan "I do need to make sure we are there or thereabouts and that is all I'm asking for."

Fair enough? Or, after the numerous issues that have befallen banks in recent years, not particularly palatable? After all, banks have been bailed out by tax-payers, they've been found guilty of manipulating interest rates and they've indulged in financial mis-selling. The banking sector ought to be a beacon of ethical rectitude but of late it has been anything but. Set against everything that has gone wrong with banks and banking, isn't lavishing £588m in bonuses a case of adding insult to injury? McEwan himself acknowledged that RBS is "the least trusted bank in the least trusted sector in the marketplace."

Moreover, what is it that banks are *actually* supposed to do? They are supposed to serve the community, to act as guardians of the citizenry's money. Yes, they are authorised to lend it – to add to the wealth of the nation. In short, banks are supposed to act for the public good. Outsize bonuses appear to have nothing to do with the public good and everything to do with personal, selfish enrichment. And if we look at the incentive argument – that huge bonuses are the carrot that inspires bankers to ever better levels of performance – it is palpably false. Academic research indicates that wage differences demotivate people; that teams of workers with even pay bands perform better. There is also evidence that recipients of big bonuses are negatively affected by extremely high pay, with the same people performing better when their pay was within more normal bounds. In fact, then, huge bonuses simply inspire greed – and contrary to the belief of the immortal Gordon Gekko, the lead character in the 1987 film *Wall Street* and its 2010 sequel, *Money Never Sleeps*, greed is not good.

Greed, indeed, could be said to have contributed to another great scandal of the early 21st century – phone hacking. In July 2011, it was revealed that the phones of murdered schoolgirl Milly Dowler, as well as victims of the 7/7 London bombings and relatives of deceased British soldiers, had been hacked by employees of the now-defunct *News of the World*, a Sunday newspaper owned by Australian media tycoon Rupert Murdoch. The outcry led to a government-driven inquiry chaired by Lord Justice Leveson, any number of high profile resignations and ultimately the trial of many journalists on charges such as conspiracy to intercept communications, perverting the course of justice, corruption, perjury and unlawful interception of messages.

At the time of writing, various trials are ongoing. Due regard for the contempt of court laws, not to mention the time-honoured presumption that an accused person is innocent until proven guilty, make for a degree of circumspection, but it is possible to make some general points.

First, sales figures and the desperation for competitive advantage clearly created what has been described as an 'endemic' culture of disregard for the law on Fleet Street. Senior journalists were happy to forget that their duty is to report truthfully and accurately and instead, in the scramble to sell the most papers, rode roughshod over morality, ethics and the law.

Secondly, albeit that there may have been a 'culture' of phone hacking, this does not make it excusable. The law actively criminalised phone hacking long before Lord Justice Leveson made many swingeing condemnations of modern-day media practice in his report. Journalists just decided to ignore the law, or worse, thought they were above it.

Finally, ethics were not merely dissonant when Milly Dowler's phone was hacked. This disgraceful and outrageous act could only have occurred in a culture of amorality – of zero ethics.

The July 2011 statement by the Ethical Investment Advisory Group (EIAG) of the Church of England, was absolutely right: "The behaviour of the *News of the World* has been utterly reprehensible and unethical." Later, in August 2012, the EIAG declared that it had no confidence in News Corporation's stated intention of returning to ethical practices. All Church of England organisations would therefore cease investment in News Corporation, which meant the Church Commissioners and the Church of England Pensions Board selling shareholdings valued at around £1.9 million. What did Rupert Murdoch, News Corp's owner, think of this? Quite possibly, he didn't care.

One person who seems not to have cared very much about ethical scruples is former Metropolitan Police forensics and surveillance officer Matt Sprake. Never heard of him? Perhaps not, but Sprake is one of the phone hacking scandal's minor characters thanks to his photography business, NewsPics. Through NewsPics, Sprake offered money to police and other public officials for information. His website continued to make the offer even as a high profile police investigation (Operation Elveden) into the alleged bribery of public officials got underway, declaring: "All sorts of people have been paid thousands of pounds by us for offering information that leads to a picture being sold or a story being written, are you a doorman, police worker, civil servant, probation officer, nurse? Make some extra money without anyone ever knowing."

Investigative news website Exaro published a story about NewsPics in July 2012, condemning its apparent disregard for ethical propriety. Sprake told Exaro that his website was "broken", and that the wording of the dubious offer should not have appeared. Sprake also said that public officials had not been paid any money – a curious position to adopt, given the clear inducement on NewsPics' website. Within hours of Exaro's story appearing, the website was miraculously fixed – and the wording removed.

So far, so sleazy – but hats off to Exaro for proving the worth and integrity of good old-fashioned journalism. But the story did not end there. Exaro had illustrated its story with two photographs of Sprake taken from the NewsPics website, which, said Sprake, were taken while he was employed by the Metropolitan Police Service. One showed him sitting at the Prime Minister's chair in No 10 Downing Street; the other showed him at the scene of the IRA's 1996 bombing in Canary Wharf, London. NewsPics advertised its services under the label, "surveillance photography", claiming: "You can utilise the very same skills that are used by the security services and the police." In using the images, Exaro was acting well within the boundaries of the law, which allows the use of material which may be owned, in copyright terms, by someone else, if that use is to expose misconduct or iniquity. Exaro's position was that it was "fair dealing" in copyright terms.

Sprake was not happy. He threatened legal action against Exaro and its reporter, the much-respected political journalist David Hencke – a threat which Exaro did not believe amounted to much. Remarkably, Sprake then went ahead and issued legal proceedings, suing for £65,000, plus £15,000 interest, for alleged breach of copyright.

Exaro remained confident of its position. The claim was a 'try-on'. Against this backdrop, Lord Justice Leveson summoned Sprake to give evidence to his inquiry into newspaper practices. Sprake defended his activities in testimony to the inquiry, but admitted that the offer of cash to public officials was a mistake. Leveson was not impressed. In his report, he condemned Sprake's ethics, calling his testimony "alarming". Leveson wrote: "Mr Sprake may prefer to call himself a photographer, but, in substance, he was a private investigator equipped with a camera."

Meanwhile, Sprake complained to the Press Complaints Commission (PCC) about the Exaro investigation as also published by The Independent. But the PCC dismissed the complaint, acknowledging the "public interest" in the story.

Sprake might, by now, have considered doing the sensible, if not right, thing and discontinuing his legal action against Exaro. But it took an application by Exaro for summary judgment to bring things to an end. Justice was finally done in September 2013 when a deputy district judge, Stuart Quin, sitting at Milton Keynes county court, threw out NewsPics' legal action. "The claims by the claimant are bound to fail," he ruled, saying that Exaro's use of the pictures plainly amounted to "fair dealing" as part of its expose.

The court ordered NewsPics to pay Exaro's costs, estimated to be in the region of £24,000. Confronted with this order, Sprake contended that NewsPics had become "technically insolvent" and had "ceased trading". NewsPics applied to dissolve itself and be struck off the company register. Exaro intervened, suspending the action, while it petitioned for a winding-up order to ensure an orderly distribution of assets owned by NewsPics.

At the time of going to press, Exaro hopes that its winding up petition will be successful. If it is, an official receiver will be appointed to sell the assets of NewsPics, in order to pay debts to Exaro and any other creditors.

Sprake and NewsPics are not 'big business'. They're bit players in the drama of phone hacking and Fleet Street's moral malaise. But they are guilty of behaving badly. The offer of money for information from public officials should never have been made; the bringing of legal proceedings was a farce that was doomed to failure. Ethically, Sprake falls short. It is open to him to do the right thing and make good Exaro's £24,000 legal bill – but this would seem to be about as likely as a UKIP politician welcoming immigrants.

Essay 5: An Unethical Personal Injury Sector

What is tolerance? It is the consequence of humanity. We are all formed of frailty and error; let us pardon reciprocally each other's folly – that is the first law of nature – Voltaire

In this, my final essay, I turn to the area of law in which I have worked since I first qualified as a solicitor – the personal injury sector. Regrettably, it is an area that is far from free of problems.

In America, the ambulance-chasing personal injury lawyer is a staple of press vilification and TV caricature. The metaphor itself goes to the heart of ethical dissonance in what ought to be a reasonably simple area of life – the business of being compensated for suffering wrongs through no fault of one's own. To imagine an injured person being ferried carefully into an ambulance, only to espy a lawyer running towards him – a lawyer intent on serving the victim, but only because there is money in it – is to behold in one fell swoop behaviour which is ethically suspect. The lawyer is capitalising on misfortune and being far too eager to profit.

In Britain the portrayal of personal injury lawyers isn't quite as negative and all-pervasive, but the business of compensation is no less fraught. Ours is the country where we have a perceived 'compensation culture', a place bedevilled by meretricious claimants and money-grabbing lawyers. The truth is otherwise, but let's examine the received 'wisdom'.

What's wrong with redress?

To read the press today, to listen to government ministers on television and radio, to type in the words 'compensation culture' to a search engine, even to spend five minutes talking to the law's arbiter of common sense (the legendary man on the Clapham omnibus) – each of these activities is to discover that Britain has a big problem with injured people obtaining redress.

Time and again, across all media, in pubs and yes, on buses, the received wisdom seems to be that we are awash with spurious claim after spurious claim. We're brainwashed into thinking that our society is crippled by manipulative scroungers on the make, by professional victims who think nothing of wildly exaggerating their injuries – if they even suffered any in the first place. We, the taxpayer, are told that we pay for the unscrupulousness of the bad apples: our car insurance premiums go up and up, our moral fibre is corroded, we can't trust anyone. Welcome to 21st century Britain and the unwelcome phenomenon of 'compensation culture', a term first coined by the late *Times* columnist Bernard Levin in an article entitled 'Addicted to Welfare' in 1993.

A report by the Better Regulation Task Force, published in May 2004, succinctly summed up the prevailing view:

> It is a commonly held perception that the United Kingdom is in the grip of a 'compensation culture'. Newspapers complain that the UK is becoming like the United States with stories of people apparently suing others for large sums of money, and often for what appear to be trivial reasons. Media reports and claims management companies encourage people to 'have a go' by creating a perception, quite inaccurately, that large sums of money are easily accessible.

And yet the report, entitled 'Better Routes to Redress', quickly went on to reveal the so-called 'compensation culture' as an urban myth. As its authors wrote: "Redress for a genuine claimant is hampered by the spurious claims arising from the perception of a compensation culture. The compensation culture is a myth; but the cost of this belief is very real."

Nearly a decade on, the tragedy is that the urban myth seems only to have become more embedded. If David Arculus and Teresa Graham, the writers of the Task Force's report, could cite any number of loaded headlines from the press in 2004 – for example, 'The culture that is crippling Britain', from the *Daily Mail*, and 'Postman sues customer who sent too many letters', from the *Daily Telegraph* – the same is true today. The most cursory scan of media analysis of this vexed subject reveals that 'Compensation culture [is] costing motorists' (from www.moneyfacts.co.uk, in February 2013) and that 'Prisoners complain about cold cells and missing cards', thanks to an inflated sense of their 'rights' as a consequence of 'compensation culture' (*The Lancashire Evening Post*, again from February 2013). The *Daily Mail* seems especially fond of stories about outlandish civil litigation claims, reporting in July 2012 on a council teacher who was allegedly "awarded thousands of pounds in damages" for stumbling over a mop and, in November the same year, regaling readers with the tale of a teaching assistant who had apparently been awarded £800,000 for a finger and elbow injury sustained when she tripped over the waist strap attached to a wheelchair. The *Mail* made its position abundantly clear: "The award, which sparked fury among war veterans and victims of crime who received substantially less for their injuries, is part of a burgeoning compensation culture among teachers who last year claimed a record £25million following accidents and employment disputes."

Many examples come squarely from the personal injury arena, but bogus notions of 'compensation culture' fuel the closely related human rights debate. As well as tabloid scaremongering blaming the banning of games of conkers from primary school playgrounds on bureaucrats from Brussels, government ministers – those should know better – like to play this game. Think especially of Theresa May's speech to the Conservative Party faithful on 4 October 2011, in which the Home Secretary excoriated the Human Rights Act for enabling an illegal immigrant to evade deportation because he owned a cat called Maya. Here is what Ms May said:

We all know the stories about the Human Rights Act. The

violent drug dealer who cannot be sent home because his daughter – for whom he pays no maintenance – lives here. The robber who cannot be removed because he has a girlfriend. The illegal immigrant who cannot be deported because – and I am not making this up – he had a pet cat.

In fact, a considered look at the judgment of Senior Immigration Judge Gleeson of December 1, 2008, presiding at an Immigration and Asylum Tribunal appeal, reveals that if May didn't think she was making up the story about the cat, she wasn't on firm factual ground. Gleeson J's ruling requires some interpretation, but its essence was clear to Justice Secretary Kenneth Clarke. Clarke was quick to say that he would be "surprised" if an illegal immigrant had persuaded the courts that he should be allowed to stay in Britain by dint of owning a cat. For good measure, he added: "In my opinion [May] should really address her researchers and advisers very severely for assuring her that a complete nonsense example in her speech was true". And so it proved: the immigrant in question was entitled to stay in the UK not because he owned a cat but because he had lived with his partner for over two years "in a genuine relationship akin to marriage."

I digress into Theresa May's notorious speech about Maya the cat to illustrate just how pervasive the tendency to misappropriate the law and its principles has become. Time and again those who should know better pedal untruths in the interests of a good soundbite or congenial headline. The result is that those who are genuinely injured, whether because of an accident or an infringement of their human rights, are made to feel that they are dining with the devil in seeking redress. But they're not. They are simply exercising a right which is fundamental part of our democracy and its evolved legal system.

Back to the beginning

Let's remember what lies behind the concept of damages in English law. The main idea behind damages for personal injury is to put the claimant in the position he or she would have been in had the accident or injury not occurred. This is something learnt by all lawyers when they study tort law. Here, we're dealing with 'ex delicto' damages. The Latin term means 'from a wrong' or 'from a transgression' (tort itself is French for 'wrong'). It's to be contrasted for damages for breach of contract ('ex contractu', for those who like their Latin words), where compensation is determined with reference to what would have happened had the contract been performed.

In other words, damages in tort law look backwards to the imaginary situation of the wrong not having happened; damages in contract look forwards to the equally imaginary position of the contract having been duly completed.

Informed by these principles, lawyers seek to assess where a victim would be, had an accident not occurred. Take, for example, an IT executive on her way to work in a car. She stops at a set of traffic lights, only to be shunted from behind by a driver who has elected to send a text message rather than watch the road ahead. It's a cut and dried case – the woman driver is innocent, the driver who hit her isn't. The lady suffers a terrible jolt to her neck. This whiplash-caused injury – simply 'whiplash' (as it is colloquially known) – is typical in such incidents; it's a simple matter of physics. Her neck hurts for days, weeks, months, making it difficult or perhaps even impossible to work or carry out everyday tasks. Understandably, she feels hard done by. Her ability to enjoy life and earn a living has been compromised, through no fault of her own. She instructs a personal injury solicitor. His task is to obtain redress for the woman which places her in the position she would be in if the accident had never occurred. A number of factors need to be considered, including the age of the claimant, the nature and extent of her injuries, gender (women generally obtain higher levels of compensation where an accident causes scarring) and personal characteristics. These are known as 'general damages'. Beyond this, the law compensates victims for what are called 'special damages' – quantifiable monetary losses. Here repair costs, replacement of property costs and loss of income will be relevant.

The law should not be used in the way which was implicit in one notorious advertisement by a claims management company. This depicted a young woman looking longingly at a sports car and saying: "I've always wanted one of those and now that I have had an accident I can have one."

But so far, so straightforward. A person is injured; that person is innocent; that person ought reasonably to be entitled to compensation. Sadly, systemic failings in the personal injury sphere now come into play. The claimant will face an uphill struggle to achieve satisfaction, especially if whiplash is suffered, because a cabal of government and insurers is intent on eliminating the existence of whiplash as a medical condition.

The essential point is this: if a victim suffers an accident, and another party is at fault, that person has the right to bring a claim. Doing so does not guarantee success. There are legal hurdles to overcome: proving that the defendant owed a duty of care, proving that the duty was breached, proving that losses were caused by the breach and that the damage sustained is not too remote. In other words, the nuts and bolts of a claim for negligence need to be present before anyone will receive any kind of compensation, and thereafter there are guidelines as to the correct level of damages (or 'quantum', as the courts call it). But to what extent are the courts taking the 'accidents just happen' view, emboldened by hysteria about the so-called compensation culture? There may be occasions when this view is appropriate and acceptable. Unfortunately, though, there is an awful lot of misinformation out there. Could it influence judicial thinking?

The spin which drives 'compensation culture'

The government was not, in 2004, persuaded by the Better Regulation

Task Force's report. In November that year, the government issued its own paper. Entitled "Tackling the 'Compensation Culture', the line from on high was abundantly clear:

> The Government is determined to scotch any suggestion of a developing 'compensation culture' where people believe that they can seek compensation for any misfortune that befalls them, even if no-one else is to blame. This misperception undermines personal responsibility and respect for the law and creates unnecessary burdens through an exaggerated fear of litigation.

Many people now believe that 'compensation culture' is alive and well – notwithstanding what ought to be the persuasive views of no less a figure than Lord Dyson, the Master of the Rolls, whose annual lecture to the Holdsworth Club (Birmingham University's student law society) stated unequivocally that we are faced with a *perceived* compensation culture, not an actual one. As to what the dread term actually means, the Better Regulation Task Force report said that it "implies that a decision to seek compensation is wrong. 'Compensation culture' is a pejorative term and suggests that those who seek to 'blame and claim' should be criticised. It suggests greed; rather than people legitimately enforcing their rights." Or, as the former minister Stephen Byers once put it: "A compensation culture of 'blame, claim and gain' is a growing threat to the public services" (*FT*, March 2004).

How, though, have we got here?

Undoubtedly, media spin is a factor (as also expressly said by Lord Dyson). Shock stories of injured claimants receiving huge amounts of money make for good copy. The more apparently outlandish the claim, the better, hence the media's delight over the infamous case of Stella Liebeck and the spilling of a cup of McDonald's coffee.

On 27 February, 1992, Mrs Liebeck, a 79-year-old woman

from Albuquerque, New Mexico, ordered a cup of coffee from the drive-through window of a McDonald's restaurant. Thereafter, sitting in the passenger seat of her grandson's stationary car, she went to add cream and sugar to her coffee. In the process, things went disastrously wrong. The coffee ended up being spilt on Mrs Liebeck's lap, scalding her thighs, buttocks, and groin. She was hospitalized for eight days and disabled for two years with third degree burns. No wonder, for the coffee had been served at 88 degrees Centigrade (190F); any temperature above 65C will cause serious burns.

Mrs Liebeck did not wish to litigate, but was forced to by McDonald's conduct. The fast-food giant dug its heels in, offering just $800 in full and final settlement when Mrs Liebeck asked for $20,000, this to cover her medical expenses and a modest loss of income. Perhaps the company had settled the 700 or so prior complaints against its super-hot coffee for sums in this region, but it came to regret its decision: at trial in August 1994, an American jury awarded damages of $160,000to cover medical expenses and compensatory damages – and $2.7 million in punitive damages. The trial judge reduced the final amount to $640,000, although that which came Mrs Liebeck's way remains confidential – the parties agreed a final figure before an appeal.

The Liebeck case was picked up by media on both sides of the Atlantic. ABC News called it "the poster child of excessive lawsuits", while Vanessa Feltz, writing in *The Daily Star*, labelled Mrs Liebeck an "American plonker who gulped her coffee and took Ronald McD to the cleaners."

This kind of sensationalism obscures the truth. The fact is that McDonald's should not have been serving coffee that was scalding hot. The potential for harm was obvious. The spilling of the coffee may have been Mrs Liebeck's fault, but she could not have expected the consequences. In all the circumstances, she had every right to sue.

Regrettably, though, a measured report of the Liebeck case – with a headline such as 'Scalded Woman Wins Damages' – would be of little interest to the majority of newspaper editors. They seem all too wedded to the well-known aphorism: 'never let the facts get in the way of a story'. This was even more evident in the notorious story about the American driver who obtained compensation when his Winnebago motor home crashed. The man had apparently left the driver's wheel to enter the motor home part of the vehicle and make a cup of coffee. He had put the vehicle on cruise control, having wrongly thought that the Winnebago's auto-pilot facility meant that it would drive himself. The result? His injuries led to an award of over $1 million – and the manufacturer rewrote the owner's manual. Needless to say, this story had any number of people jumping up and down and lamenting how 'compensation culture' was endemic in America and shortly to arrive in Britain, but it had a significant flaw: it was complete fiction. The *LA Times* estimably set the record straight in a 2005 article entitled 'Legal Urban Legends Hold Sway'.

Time for some Common Sense

The Liebeck and Winnebago cases may have set editors and journalists off on a bandwagon of claimant-bashing, but, as the Better Regulation Task Force report noted, they were soon joined by others in positions of influence, whether in government or senior public roles:

> Senior commentators, who are frequently reported, also perpetuate the perception of the 'compensation culture'. They make speeches decrying the 'compensation culture' without offering any solutions. Such speeches also give the impression that there are dual standards being applied to people litigating. Commentators are fond of criticising 'ordinary' people, but rarely criticise big companies or well-known figures for litigating. This gives the impression that there is something wrong if 'ordinary' individuals exercise their rights. People should be able to claim redress when rights have been infringed.

Absolutely so, though as an aside, it is tempting to wonder about the impact of Britain's libel laws here. Could it be that criticism of corporate lawsuits, or those brought by individuals with means, is fettered by what libel practitioners habitually call the "chilling effect" of the threat of being sued for defamation?

Undoubtedly, there are those in our society who milk their misfortune. Advertising by claims management companies and some solicitors' firms has fuelled a 'have a go and see what you might get' mentality, which, in turn, has resulted in a fear of litigation. Local councils would be negligent if they did not now factor in the possibility of claims, and a fair proportion of their annual budget goes on dealing with them. Better risk management in the first place is an obvious retort to those who say that things have gone too far, but more eloquent – in places, at least – was a report published by Lord Young, the Prime Minister's advisor on the alleged prevalence of a compensation culture as well as health and safety law and practice, on 15 October 2010. First, though, let's consider a 2002 report published by Datamonitor. Its findings chime with those of Lord Young, some eight years on.

The Datamonitor Group bills itself as "an independent, premium business information and market analysis company that assists clients with operational and strategic decision-making". It's fair to say that its reputation as a provider of business intelligence is among the best around. As such, plenty of people in the PI sector were heartened by the common sense underlying its 2002 report, entitled UK Personal Injury Litigation: The Compensation Culture Myth Exploded. Here is a Datamonitor's précis of the report:

> Fears that Britain is moving towards a US-style love of lawsuits appear unfounded. Datamonitor's new report, 'UK Personal Injury Litigation 2002' reveals that although claims for injuries have increased in frequency over the last few years, this is now beginning to tail off.

It is forecast that there will be 627,000 accident claims a year by 2007, signalling a total increase of just 2.1%. The cost of claims could be as much as GBP11 billion by 2007, meaning a GBP7.3 billion pound increase from 2002, adding further pounds to the cost of insurance.

However, the UK is not expected to imitate the US because of improvements to roads and pavements, vehicle safety and working environments reducing the number of accidents and injuries. Also compensation awards handed out in the US are much higher than in the UK, meaning that Brits are less likely to take the time for small sums of money. Finally, British people are willing to hold onto the idea of the accident, unlike the US where the blame culture is rife.

Lord Young of Graffham, himself a practising solicitor for many years, was charged with investigating 'compensation culture', alongside Britain's health and safety regime, by David Cameron while he was the leader of the opposition. Lord Young's report, entitled Common Sense, Common Safety, came out a few months after Cameron had assumed office as Prime Minister. In many ways, it appeared to echo the Datamonitor report of 2002. Take this paragraph, for example:

The problem of the compensation culture prevalent in society today is, however, one of perception rather than reality. The number of claims for damages due to an accident or disease has increased slowly but nevertheless significantly over recent years. Furthermore, there is clear evidence that the public believes that the number of claims and the amount paid out in damages have also risen significantly.

Lord Young emphasised the factors which had contributed to the perception of a compensation culture. Among them, he cited media spin, the development of 'blame culture' (in which somebody else is always at fault), the advent of Conditional Fee Arrangements (CFAs) in our civil litigation landscape, the endemic payment of referral fees and misconduct by claims management companies.

The Common Sense, Common Safety report made a number of recommendations to combat the so-called compensation culture. They included the introduction of a simplified claims procedure for PI claims similar to that which, since April 2010, had been in existence for road traffic accidents (RTA) under £10,000 on a fixed cost basis, with recommendations that extending the framework of such a scheme to cover low value medical negligence claims and increasing the upper limit for RTA PI claims to £25,000 also be explored. Beyond this, Lord Young was also clear that the recommendations made by Lord Justice Jackson in his review of civil litigation costs be implemented, so that there be greater restrictions on the payment of referral fees and the ability of claims management companies and PI law firms to advertise. Lastly, he stated that, by means of legislation if necessary, people should not be held liable for any consequences of their well-intentioned voluntary acts.

In many ways, Lord Young's rebuttal of the existence of a compensation culture was welcome. Here, at last, was an eminent figure, charged by the man who went on to become Britain's prime minister, rejecting the notion that the country was awash with spurious claims. And yet Common Sense, Common Safety itself is not a document of immaculate clarity. For example, albeit that he unequivocally stated that "compensation culture was a problem of perception rather than reality", much of Lord Young's report focuses on what he describes as the unintended consequences of the Access to Justice Act 1999. This, says Lord Young, ushered in CFAs, after-the-event (ATE) insurance and the proliferation of claims management companies, which in turn fostered "the public's increased awareness that it was possible to sue without any financial risk". Furthermore, the changes "encouraged the belief that claiming compensation for even the most minor of accidents is quick and easy, while at the same time incentivising lawyers to rack up high fees in the knowledge that they will be covered by the losing party".

On the one hand, then, Lord Young says that compensation culture doesn't exist. On the other, he fuels the belief that it is alive and well. The contradiction was articulated at a press conference to launch Common Sense, Common Safety, as reported by James Dean for *The Law Society Gazette*. As Dean wrote, on 18 October 2010:

> 'The problem of the compensation culture prevalent in society today is one of perception rather than reality,' the report states. If that is his belief, why did Young say at Friday's press conference that compensation was 'a cash cow for lawyers and referral agencies'? Why, at the Conservative party conference, did he speak of being 'ashamed' of the advertising done by personal injury firms; and why did David Cameron talk last week about 'the spectre of lawyers only too willing to pounce with a claim for damages on the slightest pretext'?

Not only did David Cameron talk about this spectre, he wrote about it, too – in the foreword to the very report in which Lord Young suggests that the so-called compensation culture is a problem of perception, not reality. "A damaging compensation culture has arisen", writes the prime minster, "as if people can absolve themselves from any personal responsibility for their own actions, with the spectre of lawyers only too willing to pounce with a claim for damages on the slightest pretext". There it is, in black and white: the belief that the compensation culture exists, and that Lord Young's review must be a "turning point".

No wonder, though, that Mr Cameron wrote and spoke as he did: Common Sense, Common Safety is rife with contradictions, and attacking the compensation culture makes for good copy. It makes him sound tough and authoritative, a man of action who believes we should all stand on our own two feet and take responsibility for whatever happens in our lives.

The truth is indeed that 'compensation culture' is myth rather than reality. Lord Dyson is absolutely correct. The term should be reclaimed, in the interests of truth and accuracy, to describe those who have no scruples, and act beyond the law. It should not be hi-jacked by lazy headline writers and politicians who prefer soundbites to facts.

What really makes for 'Compensation Culture'

Back in 2005, Tony Blair gave a speech in which he called for "common sense culture, not compensation culture". In a soundbite picked up with typical alacrity by the media, Blair said: "Public bodies, in fear of litigation, act in highly risk-averse and peculiar ways. We have had a local authority removing hanging baskets for fear that they might fall on someone's head, even though no such accident had occurred in the 18 years they had been hanging there."

Blair helped set in train a backlash against a fundamental tenet of tort law: that the claimant should, if he or she has proved negligence and causation, and if the resultant damage is not too remote, be placed in the position he or she would have been in had the accident or injury not occurred. Ever since, the media has delighted in stories of absurd claims supposedly brought by solicitors acting unethically and claimants on the make. We are told that school trips have been cancelled, for fear of accidents happening and children, through their parents, then suing, and yet, as the law firm Leigh Day found: "Research conducted by The Countryside Alliance Foundation demonstrates very clearly that of the millions of school trips taken over the past 10 years, only 364 ended in legal action and in only 156 of those cases were the schools found to be culpable. Between 1998 and 2008, the total amount of compensation paid, on average, by local authorities in relation to school trips was just £293.44 a year."

The truth is certainly contrary to media spin. The vast majority of solicitors continue to adhere to the basic principles of tort law: if someone has been injured, they take up the cudgels on that person's behalf and seek redress. They do so with the usual hurdles to overcome – proving negligence, for a start – and because it is right that our democracy allows this to happen. It is a sign that we are civilized, and that we care. Those who may need to bring claims should not fear obstruction by insurers or vilification by third parties who insist they're making the most of their misfortune. They should be emboldened in their conviction that they are entitled to right the wrongs inflicted on them.

But if we are in danger of forgetting, rather than praising, the fact that we have a developed judicial system that allows injured people to bring claims, we also live in a world where there is a truth that dare not speak its name.

Insurers are a major reason for 'compensation culture'. Their practices encourage and foster it.

It is here that ethical dissonance sounds loudest – and it is because of this that the Office of Fair Trading referred the UK's private motor insurance industry to the Competition Commission. The referral followed a study by the OFT in May 2012, which found that there were reasonable grounds to suspect that there are features of the insurance market that prevent, distort or restrict competition. In June 2014 the Commission published its provisional decision on remedies, which includes a cap on charges an insurer can pass on to the at fault driver, the provision of better information to consumers on their post-accident rights and no claims protection, a ban on price agreements between price comparison websites and insurers and stopping insurers making products available more cheaply. In September 2014 the Commission will publish its final findings; it is to be hoped that it sticks to its guns.

In a nutshell, then: there is reason to think the insurance industry is not serving its customers well.

The OFT, in its summary of the referral, put it thus: in focusing on "the provision of replacement vehicles and vehicle repairs", it was thought that "the insurers of drivers responsible for an accident ('at-fault' drivers) appear to have little control over the way repairs and replacement vehicles are provided to the 'not-at-fault' driver." The OFT added that this "may enable the insurers of not-at-fault drivers, and others such as insurance brokers, credit hire organisations and repairers, to engage in practices which appear to result in the cost of replacement vehicles and vehicle repairs provided to not-at-fault drivers being higher than they might otherwise be."

What is meant by the use of the word "practices"? Let me be clear. This means the payment of fees – which are often knowingly and deliberately inflated. The Legal Aid, Sentencing and Punishment of Offenders Act (LASPO) may have banned the flow of referral fees between solicitors, claims management companies (CMCs) and insurers, but they are alive and as insidious as ever when it comes to garages, credit hire companies leasing vehicles to drivers after accidents and recovery companies.

It's not easy to discern in the terms of the OFT referral but there is clearly a huge question mark over the conduct of insurers and their representative body, the Association of British Insurers (ABI). The ABI has proved adept at spinning the yarn that 'compensation culture' fuels hikes in insurance premiums and makes our lives a hostage to unscrupulous bounty hunters who will issue a claim at the drop of a hat – and yet it is the ABI's very members who cause the 'blame and claim' syndrome in the first place.

These thoughts lead inevitably to a consideration of the ethical standards – or absence of them – at play among insurers. Time and again stories of outlandish litigation in the media turn out to be bogus or wildly exaggerated; time and again we encounter insurers blaming the increase in the cost of premiums on everyone but themselves.

In truth, investment income – which is what our premiums are used for – has flattened out because of the global recession and so insurers seek to ramp up their profits through a back door which has become nothing but a conduit for backhanders. It's a vicious cycle: as one insurer ups the ante, passing on costs to another, so does its competitor. And so on, and on – until, hopefully, the Competition Commission will do something about it when it delivers its final report in September 2014.

Meantime, insurers continue to fall short when it comes to acting ethically. For example, a survey by CSR Europe and KPMG of five European insurers and five European banks found that 80% had no ethical objectives or targets of any kind, while only another 10% had a qualitative target.

How did we get here?

Acting for insurers, for personal injury solicitors some 20 to 30 years ago, was technically exacting and challenging. Insurer clients were knowledgeable and would quickly expose poor logic, through their own extensive experience and exposure. The task of advising on liability, quantum and tactics, with the occasional foray into procedure, was appealing to a great many litigators, including myself.

Then, on the flipside, was what it was like to be a claimant solicitor. This was even more appealing: it was a privilege to act for the claimant, an injured person, to try and obtain restitution. Solicitors love engaging in the professional evidence of others, which is so essential to bringing a personal injury claim; this, too, was one of rewards of the job.

But take a look at the legal landscape in personal injury now: from what heights we appear to have fallen. There are exaggerated claims. Aggressive marketing. Ancillary businesses, from credit hire to costs companies, are seemingly everywhere. They range from medico legal agencies to rehabilitation specialists, and they're all usually more concerned about the bottom line than about the injured people whose ill-fortune keeps them in business.

Solicitors are not exempt from charges of sharp practice. Some firms induce the making of claims where there might be none, and settle cases for their commercial benefit rather than in their client's best interest. Others string them out knowing that the longer they keep going, the more money will come in. Charles Dickens captured this regrettable aspect of legal practice perfectly in *Bleak House,* in the fictional case of *Jarndyce v Jarndyce,* a Chancery dispute that drags on for so long that the lawyers' costs devour the whole of the estate in issue. One particular passage in *Bleak House* is always worth reading:

> Jarndyce and Jarndyce drones on. This scarecrow of a suit has, in course of time, become so complicated, that no man alive knows what it means. The parties to it understand it least; but it has been observed that no two Chancery lawyers can talk about it for five minutes, without coming to a total disagreement as to all the premises. Innumerable children have been born into the cause; innumerable young people have married into it; innumerable old people have died out of it. Scores of persons have deliriously found themselves made parties in Jarndyce and Jarndyce, without knowing how or why; whole families have inherited legendary hatreds with the suit. The little plaintiff or defendant, who was promised a new rocking-horse when Jarndyce and Jarndyce should be settled, has grown up, possessed himself of a real horse, and trotted away into the other world. Fair wards of court have faded into mothers and grandmothers; a long procession of Chancellors has come in and gone out; the legion of bills in the suit have been transformed into mere bills of mortality; there are not three Jarndyces left upon the earth perhaps, since old Tom Jarndyce in despair blew his brains out at a coffee-house in Chancery Lane; but Jarndyce and Jarndyce still drags its dreary length before the Court, perennially hopeless.

Today, though, increased court management of cases and a raft of procedural changes have, thankfully, made it more and more difficult for lawyers to ape the *Jarndyce* model. Indeed, the primary problems with today's personal injury sector lie not with lawyers but with insurers.

A highly dubious landscape has come to pass, but it's time to speak up, and look at how this has come to be. It's time to take an up close and personal look at the insurance industry, where we find not just the covert encouragement of the often nonsensical 'compensation culture' spin but any number of shady practices, unprofessional conduct and unethical customs. Moreover, it transpires that insurers have a pronounced tendency to seek to control bodies that are ostensibly set up as independent.

The Motor Insurers Bureau – hijacked by the men in black?

A good place to start is with the creation of the Motor Insurers Bureau (MIB) – a classic case of insurer hi-jacking.

The MIB has been with us for quite some time now. One of the most learned commentators on the MIB, Nick Bevan, has explored its origins in depth, writing in 2011 in *The Journal of Personal Injury Lawyers*. As Bevan says: [The MIB] "plays a vital role in the framework of protective measures designed to ensure that road accident victims recover their full compensatory entitlement. The service it provides is crucial – especially for those unfortunate enough to be victims of the estimated one million (and possibly more) uninsured drivers that plague our roads. Without this safety net many injured victims would be unable to recover their compensatory entitlement because most uninsured drivers have little or no means to satisfy a judgment themselves."

So far, so good – but strip away the veneer and all is not what it seems. There are growing calls for an overhaul of the MIB, because it is not fit for purpose. A number of observers believe that what started out as a laudable and sensible initiative has become almost wholly underwritten by the insurance industry – which means that those who suffer an accident at the hands of an uninsured driver are not getting the right level of compensation.

The MIB has its genesis in the Road Traffic Act 1930. This made it obligatory for the user of a motor vehicle on a road in Great Britain to be insured against liability for personal injury caused by or arising out of that use (a requirement now contained within sections 143 to 145 Road Traffic Act 1988). As Bevan explains, almost as soon as the 1930 Act had been passed failings were noted: "The first was that many drivers were simply failing to purchase the third party motor insurance. The second problem was that even where such insurance cover existed, any material breaches by the policy holder entitled the insurer to avoid its contractual liability to indemnify. In either case, the social policy aim of ensuring that victims would recover their full compensatory entitlement from the responsible party's insurer, regardless of the financial circumstances of the defendant, was being frustrated."

Accordingly, the well-known and highly respected jurist Felix Cassel was asked to investigate matters. He chaired the Board of Trade committee on compulsory insurance from 1935 to 1937. In 1937, the Cassel Committee made two key recommendations: one, that there should be further legislation to regulate motor insurance contracts more stringently, and two, that a National Guarantee Fund should be set up to compensate victims of uninsured drivers.

Before the Fund could be set up by the government, along came the Second World War. But in its aftermath insurers seized the initiative, proposing a statutory scheme that insurers would administer (a tactic which is now all too familiar). This, then, is how the MIB came into being on 1 July 1946 – as a private company, established to allow the motor insurance industry to contract with the state to deliver a compensatory scheme for victims of negligent uninsured and untraced motorists. The MIB then implemented a succession of schemes, beginning with the Uninsured Drivers Agreement 1946 (modified in 1972, 1988 and 1999). It also created the Untraced Drivers Agreement in1969, updating this to its current form in 2003.

In 1973, Britain's entry into the European Community made for a fresh set of European obligations. There are many reasons to doubt the MIB's compliance with them, but the key issue is the way in which the MIB has evolved – and the power it now wields. As can be seen from how it came into being, it is not the product of altruism or largesse. Today it is an impressive, and large, organisation: as Bevan notes, "In 2009, MIB employed about 320 staff and handled approximately 60,000 uninsured and untraced driver claims from its premises in Milton Keynes." It has gone on to pursue any number of commercial activities both here and in Europe, paid for by the public. Bevan again succinctly summaries what we have got, in the form of the MIB: "every penny expended by the MIB in satisfying claims under the Uninsured and Untraced Drivers Agreements and in managing the seemingly ever widening role of the MIB is eventually recouped from the premium paying public. The State has in effect empowered the representative body of a commercial consortium to impose indirect taxation in order to implement its social policy aims."

Today's MIB, then, is not quite as straightforward as insurers would have us believe (indeed, its procedures are so Byzantine as to symbolise powerfully everything that is wrong with it). It is as if it has been designed to confound and obfuscate.

If major insurers control the MIB, and the compulsory provision of insurance, what else do they control? Quite a lot, is the unfortunate answer.

The claims portals: portals to the insurers' best interests

Another instance of insurers' preoccupation with control – dressed up as something for the injured person's good – comes in the form of insurers' approach to the various Claims Portals that have come into being in recent years. The Ministry of Justice, as part of the seemingly endless drive to reform the civil litigation landscape (until, perhaps, there are no claims left, or so a cynic might say) decreed that Road Traffic Act (RTA) claims of up to £10,000 in value ought to be conducted via a new pre-action protocol, and routed and managed through a new electronic Claims Portal. This meant the swift electronic processing of claims – and their quicker settlement (a laudable objective). The first portal, for claims under the RTA, was set up in 2010. It was followed by another portal again dealing with so-called 'low value' claims (now set at up to £25,000), those involving Employer Liability (EL) and Public Liability (PL), set up in July 2013.

These kinds of claim make up the bread and butter of personal injury claims. They're not glamorous – if 'glamour' can ever be said to accrue to claims which only arise because someone has been injured – but they're vitally important. They affect a vast number of people; people who have been injured, and need legal representation to obtain redress. Initiatives to speed up claims of this nature are welcome; the notion of a fast track is good. But what's not so welcome is the way in which insurers try to control the portals, from their administration to questions of over-arching policy.

Perhaps one thing distils this better than any other – the fact that claimant representatives were kept in the dark by insurers and the government during the creation of the portals. At the outset, what should have been an amalgam of stakeholders saw insurers, and insurers alone, select the management company for the first portal. Management of the first portal was by an insurance sub-contractor and then moved to a wholly owned subsidiary of the MIB – which, as we have seen, is an organisation controlled by insurers. What is now Claims Portal Ltd, a not-for-profit company comprised of 13 non-executive directors, including an independent chairperson. The directors represent the Association of Personal Injury Solicitors (APIL), the Motor Accident Solicitors Society (MASS), the TUC, the Law Society, the MIB and, of course, insurers. While its board is balanced between claimant and compensator directors it remains the case that he who pays the piper calls the tune, added to which the portals are managed by staff of the MIB. To date the claims portal remains funded by insurers notwithstanding a joint venture agreement to move to a different system in which users pay, which would mean de facto freedom from insurer control in terms of funding. At the time of going to print, some progress to user pays (away from insurer funding control) is being made – a full four years after it was agreed to move to the user pays model.

I was an inaugural claimant representative, serving as a director representing MASS and continuing in that capacity until April 2012, when I became Vice-President of the Association of Personal Injury Lawyers. I can say with authority, then, that the committed Claims Portal Board has gone a significant way towards ensuring a balanced approach. However, implementing the user, rather than insurer pays, model is a necessary and overdue further step.

In addition, insurers have lobbied for the portals to be extended and, at the same time, for recoverable legal costs for claims in the portals to be driven down – to date, with great success. The financial limit for claims has risen from £10,000 to £25,000; recoverable costs have been slashed by up to 58%. The result is inimical to justice, turning claims into commodities – and very low value ones at that. It is commercially unviable for many solicitors even to contemplate acting for a claimant in portal claims – and that's just how the insurers like it. But the truth is this: these kinds of small claim are what happens *in life*. Thankfully, the majority of us have to find solicitors to handle injuries from which we will recover, in time, rather than catastrophic, life-changing injuries. However, everything is relative: awards up to £25,000 (the upper limit in the portals) include injuries of significant and permanent impact. With a young person on the minimum wage earning not much over £7,500, a claim up to £25,000 is a huge amount of money, and of commensurate significance. Given the importance of these claims, surely the body administering them should be truly independent?

The cancer of referral fees

I can vividly recall giving evidence on Tuesday 10 October 2011 to House of Commons Transport Committee, which sat to take oral evidence on the rising cost of motor insurance. It was the second time I'd attended a select committee meeting. In November 2010, I gave evidence before Louise Ellman MP, who is the very able chair of the Commons Transport Select Committee. Then, as now, I found that the experience of engaging with Parliament has its Kafkaesque moments.

As in the Czech novelist's great novel, *The Trial* – which sees Joseph K search fruitlessly for justice, having been arrested for a reason that is never specified – the splendour of the surroundings is inescapable. The Palace of Westminster, which is where I also gave evidence in 2010, is awe-inspiring, both in its sense of history and architecture. Portcullis House, where the 10 October 2011 hearing took place, is rather less grand but still has an august flavour, perhaps because of its name: it is so called after the chained portcullis used to symbolise the Houses of Parliament on letterheads and official documents.

But for all the grandeur, the business of actually appearing to give evidence isn't easy. In 2010, it seemed as if I was asked to wait interminably outside an apparently limitless number of doors, rather than be ushered directly to the Committee. It was only by dint of determination that I managed to find the room in the Palace of Westminster in which the Committee was sitting. In 2011, the venue had changed (from the Palace to Portcullis House) at the last minute – but no one thought to tell me. It's almost as if because everyone within Parliament knows the drill, they forget to tell the rest of us.

Jack Straw MP, the former Lord Chancellor and Secretary of State, is a man who knows Parliament like the back of his hand. Perhaps this gave him the confidence to breeze into the hearing a few minutes after it had started; certainly, I was in the midst of introducing myself when he arrived.

Attending a hearing in the company of a heavy hitter such as Jack

Straw means that one has to be determined to be heard. Fortunately, my previous Select Committee experience stood me in good stead. Representing MASS as I then was, I felt I made MASS's point: that unless the Government tackles systemic failings within the personal injury industry, its proposed ban on referral fees alone may do more harm than good.

At around this point, I was conscious of a curious atmosphere. Portcullis House seemed possessed of uncertainty. And then I realised: the MPs to whom I and others were giving evidence simply had no idea of the extent of dysfunction of the personal injury and motor insurance market when it came to referral fees. Granted, the Ministry of Justice was, at this time, proposing a ban on them, but the nitty-gritty of what went on by way of metaphorical brown envelopes was almost entirely unknown to the world at large.

Extraordinarily – or not, depending on the extent of one's cynicism – insurers knew full well about referral fees – after all, they were the ones paying them – and yet said nothing. The system was rife with corruption. As I gave evidence to the Committee, it would be a fair bet to suggest that somewhere in the country a personal injury lawyer was signing off a payment which secured drivers' details from an insurer, a garage or, most probably, a claims management company. En route, data protection laws would almost certainly have been breached – customers almost certainly *didn't* really consent, when they had that minor, now happily forgotten accident a couple of years ago, for their mobile phone numbers to end up on an accident claim marketer's database. The bottom line was this: backhanders were everywhere – and insurers were actually selling claims to solicitors.

No wonder that Lord Justice Jackson, in his Review of Civil Litigation Costs, described the paying of referral fees as "abhorrent". No surprise that the Chairman of the Bar, Peter Lodder QC, agreed wholeheartedly. For him, referral fees were "bribes and add an unnecessary cost to litigation ... [they have] no place in a fair and open justice system." More to the point, selling claims for fees means, inevitably, that claims will be made. And yet who makes the loudest noise about the so-called 'compensation culture', and who asks its clients to pay ever-bigger premiums?

The Ministry of Justice went on to ban referral fees – a good move, albeit one that was rushed through, poorly executed and left plenty of loopholes. For their part insurers, having played dumb initially, performed a volte face when they realised the cat was out of the bag, themselves calling for reform and playing the 'everyone's at it' card (as if to say, 'what choice did we have? We only played the game because we had to.'). Reform, though, was bitter-sweet: along came the Alternative Business Structure (ABS), much trumpeted following the passing of the Legal Services Act 2007 and duly authorised by the Solicitors Regulation Authority. ABSs came formally into being in early 2012 and set the scene for a revolution in the way solicitors run their businesses, allowing non-lawyers to own and invest in law firms. The media tended to focus on the 'Tesco law' implications of this – understandably, for can a Tesco conveyancing service, predicated on high volume transactions conducted at breakneck speed, match that of the traditional conveyancing solicitor? But there was another, just as worrying and arguably more insidious aspect to the brave new ABS regime. Put simply, insurers and claims management companies could now own law firms. Howzat for a way round the referral fee ban? And meantime, the raft of ancillary fees paid by those outside the legal profession – the likes of medico-legal companies, garages, reporting engineers and towing companies – continued unbridled. These bodies all habitually pay referral fees; to date, they are not properly regulated.

Pre-medical offers: another surprise for the Transport Committee

Summer 2013 saw the publication of the eagerly anticipated report by the cross-party House of Commons Transport Committee on the cost of motor insurance. As one would hope and expect, a number of sensible points were made. There was, though, a sentence that stood out. It illustrated the endemic malpractice in the insurance sector:

> MPs on the committee were surprised to find that insurers sometimes made an offer to personal injury claimants even before they had received their medical report.

The MPs may have been surprised – incredulous, in truth – but those of us working at the coalface in the personal injury sector have long objected to the practice of what is laughably known as 'third party assistance'.

Third party assistance happens when insurers make direct contact with people who have potential claims. According to the Association of British Insurers (which has a voluntary code for its members on the practice), insurers contact people in this way for benign reasons. As the ABI put it in 2009, in a statement which, at the time of writing, remains on its website:

"If an insurer contacts an injured third party it will be to ensure that they get fair compensation and the best possible rehabilitative care more quickly than through the legal process. In doing so, insurers will ensure that the person is fully aware of their legal rights and options.

"The FSA's guidance, combined with our own code of practice which we will be publishing shortly will ensure that claimants get the best possible deal as quickly as possible. It will also reduce legal costs, which all customers end up paying for through higher premiums."

Does this bear scrutiny? Hardly. In fact, not to put too fine a point on it, the notion of 'third party assistance' – something practised by insurers for the greater good – is ridiculous. What actually happens in third party assistance is that an injured person is contacted by an insurer before he or she has obtained legal advice, and before any medical evidence exists. If conducted skilfully by an insurer's representative, the ensuing phone call means that an injured person's claim is settled in the absence of a medical report as to the extent and ramifications of the injuries – and before legal advice has been obtained. As such, while third party assistance might result in a quick cash fix, it only ever renders justice and better rehabilitative care inadvertently. Its sole aim is to buy off claims cheaply and before the injured person instructs a lawyer.

The insurance industry hated it, but the Law Society hit the nail on the head with its 'Don't get mugged by an insurer' advertising campaign in 2013. Law Society research showed that people who seek a solicitor's advice receive two to three times more compensation than those who accept an insurer's first offer. Insurers contend this is down to the bogus notion of 'compensation culture', that we live in a society where everyone is on the make, but it is their very conduct in the first place that fuels this. If they insist on ringing people up as soon as there's an accident, they create, by word of mouth, the expectation that there must be some money to be had.

Among its recommendations, the Transport Committee urged insurers to put their own house in order. Needless to say, insurers have carried on exactly as before, making pre-medical offers under the guise of 'assistance' and, into the bargain, trying to find a scapegoat. That which sprang most obviously to their attention was whiplash (a colloquial term to describe soft tissue injuries to the spine), a painful and debilitating condition for anyone unfortunate enough to suffer it but, to insurers, a myth. James Dalton, the ABI's head of motor and liability, summed up the insurer perspective in March 2014, calling for damages for whiplash to be abolished altogether (suggesting instead that claimants should have their rehabilitation paid for). Worse, insurer-driven spin has been swallowed hook, line and sinker by the government (one wonders why), with the result that higher premiums are blamed on Britain having become 'the whiplash capital of the world'. Because so many of us are rushing to solicitors' offices and issuing proceedings at the merest twinge in our necks, the poor, beleaguered and altruistic insurance industry has no choice but to put up its premiums.

As it happens, whiplash exists. It hurts. And more to the point, the latest statistics from the Compensation Recovery Unit (a civil service department which has been collating annual statistics on the number of claims made each year for over 20 years) show that whiplash claims are actually *falling*. That ought to be good news for everyone, but it isn't for insurers: at this rate they might have to look in the mirror and confess that what they see isn't very pleasant. In any event, they'll need another scapegoat. Anyone for mesothelioma?

Mesothelioma – a death sentence which insurers do nothing to ameliorate

Mesothelioma is an asbestos-related cancer. Approximately 2,200 people currently die in England and Wales each year from the disease, with sufferers having an average life expectancy of only seven to nine months from diagnosis. Some 50% of claims for compensation for mesothelioma take over 12 months to settle, which means that sufferers may die before their claims are paid out.

The government acted to help mesothelioma victims by introducing the Mesothelioma Bill in 2012, which was passed as the Mesothelioma Act in 2014. Its aim was laudable: to provide compensation for sufferers of mesothelioma by setting up a lump-sum payment scheme funded by insurers to meet claims where the original insurer is untraceable. The Act will therefore establish a mesothelioma payments scheme as well as guidance about the resolution of certain insurance disputes for those affected by mesothelioma. Its introduction was long overdue, given what we know about mesothelioma: that it is a disease caused by exposure to asbestos, with a long delay between exposure and developing the disease (often 40 to 50 years). It is nearly always fatal. Over the years sufferers have faced a massive battle to obtain compensation, owing either to the difficulty of tracing employers or, indeed, insurers. Hence, then, the sensible and commendable advent of the Mesothelioma Act (though it is regrettable to note that the scheme would only pay out 75%, not 100%, of the dying person's claim).

But the Act was manipulated by insurers in the most subtle and underhand fashion. Even insurers know they can't contend that mesothelioma sufferers are malingerers or fantasists, as they say of whiplash sufferers. But they could look into their crystal balls and see an awful lot of money going into mesothelioma claims. How, then, to stop this happening?

The answer came in the form of a government consultation on the pre-action protocol for mesothelioma – which led to a government U-turn. In its wisdom, uninfluenced, of course, by insurers, the government decided to revoke the exemption of mesothelioma claims from the irrecoverability of the success fee and after the event premium elements on behalf of such claimants under the Legal Aid, Sentencing and Punishment of Offenders Act 2012 (LASPO). What does this mean, in plain English? It means that mesothelioma sufferers – people who are dying – have to pay for the inherent risks of legal action (a consequence that is now subject to a judicial review). Callously, this was presented by the ABI and the government as advantageous to claimants, because it enables them to enjoy an additional 10% in damages, knowing full well that this does not begin to compensate for the loss of recoverability. Thanks to this sinister bit of behind-the-scenes manoeuvring by insurers, those subject to the death sentence of mesothelioma have extra stress and anxiety in their last few months alive – and they may well die before their claim even gets off the ground.

On Valentine's Day in 2012, there was a motor premium summit of insurers and the government at 10 Downing Street. The guest list was impressive, with any number of figureheads from the insurance sector including Association of British Insurance director general Otto Thoresen, Aviva UK chief executive Trevor Matthews and Axa UK CEO Paul Evans. Remarkably, though, not a single claimant solicitor, representative or claimant was present. None was invited.

This little love-in tells us a lot about the ethical standards underpinning the insurance sector – itself the primary cause of our so-called 'compensation culture', willingly aided and abetted by those with vested interests, aka, the government.

Conclusion

Integrity has no need of rules – Albert Camus, The Myth of Sisyphus (1942)

In these essays I've taken a broad brush view of various sectors of society. I started with sport and followed it with entertainment because these two areas are so accessible. Then I took a look at MPs and the police, before moving on to the business world and then concluding with a slightly more detailed consideration of the sector I know best (having worked in it most of my life), personal injury.

Throughout my intention was not to provide a minute and forensic analysis, still less to anchor my essays to a particular philosophic or ethical standpoint. I am the last person to claim academic expertise in such rarefied matters. I am simply an ordinary person, a solicitor by trade, who – like a great many other people – looks on at a myriad of conduct by people who occupy positions of trust and responsibility in public life and finds their lack of a moral compass to be both deeply worrying and dismaying.

As such, the quote by Albert Camus, above, informs this book. "Integrity has no need of rules", writes the French novelist and philosopher (and accomplished goalkeeper). He is right. Not dissimilarly, Winston Churchill once observed that "If you have ten thousand regulations you destroy all respect for the law." The point is plain. I believe that history has taught us how to behave; that there are embedded norms and mores that have become part of the fabric of society, by means of the influence of religion, the operation of the rule of law and the development, in many countries, of democracy. Again, please allow this broad overview, but what I am saying is this: we *know* how to behave, how to do right by our fellow human beings, what *not* to do. But time and again people behave less than correctly, and when they do, the clarion call is for greater regulation, changes in the law, yet more checks and balances.

We don't need them. We need society to put a premium on behaving ethically. We need to educate our children so that they understand the value and good sense in acting ethically, in treating their peers decently, in not seeking to get one over on them or capitalise unthinkingly on their errors or perceived weaknesses.

So, in sport, while we can and should celebrate the mavericks, we shouldn't turn a blind eye to professional fouls or give a pat on the back to the sportsperson who cheats to gain an advantage for self and team. Imagine how different life would be, if our children watched commentators on sports programmes (who are almost always former sportspeople) condemn cheating rather than tacitly condone it.

It is easy, and right, to castigate a Lance Armstrong – a callous and cynical cheat who betrayed the trust of so many and whose apology was hollow and meaningless. It is less easy, and takes more courage, to stand up and say that, in football for example, the professional foul is wrong. An even braver pundit may yet emerge and declare that the player whose match-winning handball or dive is not seen by the referee has committed a wrong not just against the opposing team but, however subtly, against society.

In the world of entertainment, programmes such as *The Apprentice* make for compulsive viewing. But so too do they endorse amorality at best, immorality at worst. How much better would it be to watch a show like *The Apprentice* and see that serial ethical offenders do not prosper, that they are doomed from the moment their 'win at all costs, trample anyone who gets in the way' mentality first surfaces? What a relief it would be to encounter candidates who declared that they wanted to work with Sir Alan Sugar because doing so would give them a platform not to bid for an appearance, one day, in the *Sunday Times Rich List* but because it was the best way they could do good in the world.

Is this naïve? I don't think so. And nor is it naïve to expect better of our police force and our politicians. It is not good enough that we have come to expect that "something is rotten" in institutions like the police and parliament. We need, in these arenas, people of integrity – not MPs who are on the make, happy to take bribes to feather their nests, still less police officers who think nothing of manipulating the truth or being racist. We need people who have the moral fibre of the late Sir Robin Cook, whose principles meant that he resigned from his positions as Lord President of the Council and Leader of the House of Commons on 17 March 2003 in protest against the invasion of Iraq. We need a wholesale recommitment to the Nolan Principles, so that selflessness in public office becomes second nature – not just a box to be ticked by way of currying favour with the public.

Big business can and must do better, too. A great many corporations and professional services firms now have discernible corporate responsibility policies. In some cases, these will have been adopted cynically, again by way of ticking a box that has to be ticked. But in a many others big business has at last understood that fleecing the customer in search of profit is not the way forward. By all means work hard, develop strategies to drive the business forward – but you don't have to ride roughshod over human beings (whether staff, customers or competitors) en route. Or, as Melinda Gates memorably put it: "Helping people does not have to be an unsound financial strategy."

And finally to the law and, specifically, the personal injury sector. "What is law, for us?" asks Socrates, the Ancient Greek philosopher, in *Minos* by Plato. He goes on to elaborate on the meaning of the law in a complex fashion, saying that the law "wishes to be the discovery of what is". As I understand it Socrates was making the point that the law is something *discovered* by legislators; as such, it must be fit for purpose; it must suit human society. Or, as Socrates put it: "Law is the *correct* judgment of the state." Martin Luther King puts flesh on the bones of this in his observation: "Never forget that everything Hitler did was legal."

Our legislators must act so as to find the right laws for us. And a great many laws have, in truth, been found. We privilege, rightly, the rule of law, and yet we only have to look at the phone hacking scandal to see just how flagrantly laws – perfectly good, sensible laws – can be disregarded.

Why? Because profit meant too much. It was more important to get the best story and outsell competitors than to report fairly and accurately and act in an ethical way. And nowhere does the endemic ethical dissonance in modern society sound as loudly as in the personal injury sector, where, as I have shown, backhanders abound, the cancer of referral fees is everywhere and insurers play the 'everyone's at it' card – a card that cynically justifies their own behaviour. It's a card that no one should play but more to the point, when was it ever ethical to vilify injured people, as insurers insist on doing? If someone is injured through no fault of their own, but because of the fault of another, we should extend sympathy for them and encourage them to seek compensation, if the circumstances allow. Instead, insurers demonise the injured and falsely claim that their bogus creation of the 'compensation culture' is why car premiums continue to rise.

Finally, to return to the law, just as I was concluding this book the unedifying spectacle of Constance Briscoe and her perversion of the course of justice hit the headlines. What an extraordinary and depressing case: here was a barrister and part-time judge who was prepared to lie to the police, falsify a witness statement and provide a false document to an expert witness, all to assist her friend Vicky Pryce in the no less scandalous case of Pryce and Chris Huhne's own attempt to pervert the course of justice. Thankfully, the arrogant trio of Pryce, Huhne and Briscoe were all convicted; as I was concluding this book Briscoe was starting a 16-month jail term. As the judge in the Briscoe trial put it: if Briscoe, Huhne and Pryce shared anything in common it was "arrogance by educated individuals who considered respect for the law was for others." The judge added: "I am sure that you realise only too well that such conduct strikes at the heart of our much-cherished system of criminal justice, which is integral and invaluable to the good order of society."

Briscoe, of course, is the author of a best-selling memoir entitled *Ugly*. Its claims have been disputed by Briscoe's family from the start; witnessing her daughter's fall from grace, Briscoe's own mother said: "She should have been in the dock a long time before now… She is a first-class liar…" It is even possible that some, if not all, of Briscoe's judgments will now be appealed; whether there will ever be a rapprochement between her and her mother is less certain.

What, then, proved to be truly ugly is a barrister's contempt for the very legal system that gave her a career.

Ethically, Briscoe lost her way. She is far from alone; far too many people, in roles of responsibility and importance, choose to do likewise. But in doing so they tarnish not only themselves but the rest of us.

And to look at the case of Constance Briscoe is to apprehend, in one fell swoop, that we don't need a new set of rules, or an enquiry, or a government think-tank to ponder and declaim from on high; we don't need fresh legislation and we don't need to reinvent the wheel. The wheel is sound; it turns well; it serves us all: but it needs a thorough servicing. The cogs of our society need an ethical stock-take; our leaders need to take their courage in both hands and remind us of the value of sound ethical principles, of behaving well, of acting decently, of caring for and looking after our fellows, whether they're friends or people we've never met.

To return to Wilde and *The Importance of Being Earnest,* being 'earnest' meant inhabiting a world of false truths, smugness and complacency, a world in which so long as things *appear* to be alright, then they must *be* alright. This has come to be our world, in far too many ways. But to look under the surface, in the arenas of sport and entertainment to politics, business, the law and beyond, things *aren't* always alright. In fact, too often they're downright wrong – in a way that we simply *know* to be wrong.

Things are a long way from the conduct of a shining exemplar like Jesse Owens, a man whose whole life and legacy tell us that it is, after all, important to be ethical. But they needn't be. As the inspirational Anne Frank put it: "How wonderful it is that nobody needs to wait a single moment before starting to improve the world."

There is an importance to being ethical. It's one that we're in danger of losing, and it's one that we would all do well to embrace.

THE END

Acknowledgements

I would like to thank the following people for their help in connection with this book:

Alex Wade for writing it, refining it, arguing it; moreover his friendship.

Nick Bevan for his fine work and unparalleled expertise and enthusiasm to unearth all mysteries of the MIB.

Charo Garzon-Melero, from whom I learned the importance of aligning belief and action throughout my work and family life, and beyond.

Gavin Ingham Brooke, and his team at Spada (not least Scott Addison and Rob Bownes) with whom I and colleagues at Spencers worked to refine our ethical approach to clients and business.

Alex Kane and Beth Farrer for their continuing support.

Our Board at Spencers – Rob Landman, Martyn Gilbert, and Jane Gittins, true and honourable people and friends from whom I have learnt so much about a calling higher than commerce or money. Their sense of community and employment responsibility has returned tenfold whatever leadership I have been privileged to provide to them. Thanks also to past board member and friend, Allison O'Reilly, who always led and supported a higher cause.

Susanne, my dear wife and best friend always. To Joe and Esme my dear children who have always kept my feet on the ground. To dear Lydia, our daughter, who passed on to a better place, on the 7th May 2014. Lydia taught me so much about life and care and adventure and joy. She was someone who knew what matters most and always gave it priority. Our loss and heaven's gain. Amen.